"His heart and honesty are like a gu[...] [...]ing Christian who has spent their ch[...] for the show. His naked disregard for the kind of pretense and posturing that has turned off so many hurting people is refreshing and should be emulated by others wherever and whenever possible. That includes me."

BRIAN, ATTORNEY, CALIFORNIA

"I picked up *Dare to Drop the Pose* wondering what I could *really* learn from a 'big-shot megachurch pastor' whose life was *obviously* one big success story. What God did in my heart truly shocked me. As I read through Craig's confessions, I came face-to-face with my own struggles and was confronted with one lingering question: If a publicly successful pastor can openly confess his greatest weaknesses, surrender them to God, and experience this kind of freedom, what am I waiting for? This book will challenge you to get real about your faults, while launching you on a journey to uncover strengths you never knew you had."

AARON B., WEB DESIGNER, OKLAHOMA

"Craig holds nothing back as he reveals all. Finally, someone who has the guts to be real. I found it easy to relate to Craig's life experiences: many were funny, yet all were profound. I've been inspired and challenged to be honest with myself and God."

CHRIS P., ENTREPRENEUR, AUSTRALIA

"*You've got to be kidding me.* That's what I thought as I read *Dare to Drop the Pose. Can he really be that honest?* Thanks, Craig, for leading the way. Now, I think I can be more honest with my wife, my kids, and my church."

"This book comes at you like an Oklahoma lightning storm on a hot summer day. I thought I was honest, open, transparent, and confident enough in my fiftieth year to speak the truth about who I am and how I feel without being concerned with what people may think. I was wrong! The truth is, I have never been *totally* honest with *anybody*, not my boss, not my best friend, not my family, not even my spouse. Today is the day of change!"

"My perfectionist standards have been trampled, and God's Word has bandaged the wounds of those lies. I can't wait to see how God will use the 'real' me."

"Craig not only addresses the topics that most Christians are scared to talk about, but more importantly tells us what God says about them. As a fellow Christ follower, Craig's vulnerability in this book is very refreshing."

CRAIG GROESCHEL

DARE
TO
DROP
THE
POSE

Ten Things Christians Think but Are Afraid to Say

MULTNOMAH
BOOKS

DARE TO DROP THE POSE
PUBLISHED BY MULTNOMAH BOOKS
12265 Oracle Boulevard, Suite 200
Colorado Springs, CO 80921

All Scripture quotations, unless otherwise indicated, are taken from the Holy Bible, New International Version®. NIV®. Copyright © 1973, 1978, 1984 by International Bible Society. Used by permission of Zondervan Publishing House. All rights reserved. Scripture quotations marked (NLT) are taken from the Holy Bible, New Living Translation, copyright © 1996. Used by permission of Tyndale House Publishers Inc., Wheaton, Illinois 60189. All rights reserved. Scripture quotations marked (NKJV) are taken from the New King James Version®. Copyright © 1982 by Thomas Nelson Inc. Used by permission. All rights reserved.

ISBN 978-1-60142-314-6
ISBN 978-0-307-56223-4 (electronic)

Published in the United States by WaterBrook Multnomah, an imprint of the Crown Publishing Group, a division of Random House Inc., New York.

MULTNOMAH and its mountain colophon are registered trademarks of Random House Inc.

Library of Congress Cataloging-in-Publication Data
Groeschel, Craig.
   Confessions of a pastor / by Craig Groeschel.
      p. cm.
   1. Groeschel, Craig. 2. Clergy—United States—Biography. 3. Christian life.
I. Title.
   BR1725.G92A3 2006
   277.3'083092—dc22
   [B]   2006019252

Printed in the United States of America
2010—First Edition

10 9 8 7 6 5 4 3 2 1

SPECIAL SALES
Most WaterBrook Multnomah books are available at special quantity discounts when purchased in bulk by corporations, organizations, and special-interest groups. Custom imprinting or excerpting can also be done to fit special needs. For information, please e-mail SpecialMarkets@WaterBrookMultnomah.com or call 1-800-603-7051.

Table of Contents

I Had Been Living a Lie

One Sunday, I stood before my church, filled with fear. Fear that they would think I had failed them as their pastor, that I had let them down. But I was finally ready to tell the truth—I was sure it was what God wanted me to do.

I hadn't had an affair or stolen from the church funds. In fact, my sins were small, everyday things; they were all just hidden from view. From the pews, it looked as if I had become everything and done everything a pastor should— and I worked very hard to keep it that way. I had *played* the part to perfection.

And that was the problem.

I'm going to share the story of an impostor exposed. It's more than the story of one Sunday morning, though. It's about how, over a lifetime, a reasonably well-intentioned follower of

Jesus can succeed at building an impressive exterior but fail miserably at being the real thing—the person God so lovingly created in the first place.

You may not like me after reading this book. But on the chance God might use my story to help you put down the masks and reclaim the real you, it's a risk I'm willing to take.

FACTORS THAT MADE THE ACTOR

From my earliest childhood memories, I remember "playing the game." Maybe you played it, too. I'd try to say the right things at the right times to the right people. When the people or circumstances changed, so did I.

As a young child, I tried my best to please my parents. In school I made sure my teachers got my grandest act. There's nothing terribly wrong with that, but looking back, I see that those were just practice runs for what would come later.

As a teenager I did almost anything for acceptance from my buddies. I partied, swore, lied, cheated, and stole. I thought these things would help my popularity. Whether that lifestyle gained me friends is debatable. What it could have cost me in the long run is not. By the time I started college, I was playing so many different roles that I began to lose track of the "real me." Honestly, I began to wonder if there *was* a real me.

At nineteen I became a follower of Christ. And the parts of my life He changed, He changed miraculously. He cleaned house. But in a darkened corner here, a locked closet there, I continued to believe I was better off putting up a front. Except now it was a new front, a spiritual one. It was still the same old game, just played out on a different stage.

Within a few years, I became a pastor. You'd think that becoming "a man of the cloth" (whatever that means) would have shaken the deceit right out of me. But as a young pastor, I simply turned pro. My church members observed my finest performances. And I fooled many of them, but I didn't fool myself…

And I didn't fool God.

I entered seminary *after* I had been a pastor for a while. One of my professors taught me many invaluable ministry principles. In fact, I still practice most of what I learned from him, and I'm eternally grateful for his friendship and leadership. However, one of the things he shared with me I now believe was not only wrong, but incredibly dangerous. He called it the "pastor's mystique." And he told us ministry trainees that we had to guard it at all cost.

"People think they want their pastors to be *normal, every-day people*," he used to tell our class, "but they really don't. They want to see you as superhuman, better than the average person. Church members want to believe your marriage is always strong, your faith never falters, and you are virtually without sin."

I hung on every word, soaking up his advice.

Week after week, my professor returned to his warnings about a pastor's mystique: "Keep your guard up," he'd say. "Don't let them know the real you. Always dress the part. Always talk the part. You're a pastor now. And you can never let them into your life. Or you'll regret it."

This sounded logical to me. He'd obviously been deeply wounded in his ministry and wanted to help us avoid similar pain. I knew then—and still believe—that he meant well. So I took what he said to heart and continued perfecting my "good pastor" act. I'd smile big at the church members, shake each hand with *both* of mine, and end each conversation with the pastor's best line: "God bless you." Somewhere on my journey, though, I forgot that God called me...not to be *like a pastor*, but to be *like Christ*.

That's when my spiritual struggles started. I wasn't living with gross, unconfessed sin—at least not the kind that gets pastors fired. And my motives weren't bad. I loved Jesus and His people. Every bone in my body desired to make a difference for God in this world. I poured my heart fully into ministry, enduring long hours, boring meetings, grueling classes, temperamental people, and plenty of good, old-fashioned church conflicts—all for Jesus.

After a few years, I became *good* at being a pastor. Ministerial words flowed from my mouth. I learned what to say and what not to say. Weddings were a breeze, and funerals were becoming easier. Preaching came naturally, and my counseling skills gradually improved. Most people said I was an "up 'n' comer," the kind of pastor who'd rise quickly through the ranks to a bigger church. From the outside, everything looked good.

But God doesn't look at the outside.

THE FIRST OF MANY CONFESSIONS

One Sunday, after another week of performing my best for God, I stood to preach His life-changing Word. As I approached the pulpit, the truth hit me squarely between the eyes. I hadn't prayed at all. Not that day. Not the day before. Not the day before that. To the best of my knowledge, I hadn't prayed all week.

And I called myself a pastor. That's when it dawned on me: *I had become a full-time minister and a part-time follower of Christ.* From the outside, I looked the part. "God bless you," I'd say, followed by the promise, "I'll be praying for you."

But that was usually a lie.

Stepping onto the platform to preach that morning, I admitted to myself that I was not a pastor first, but a regular, scared, insecure, everyday guy whose life had been changed by Jesus. And if Jesus really loved me as I was (I knew He did), then why should I go on trying to be someone I wasn't?

I stumbled through that sermon, forcing the words to come out. The message was superficial, plastic, shallow…but somehow I got through it. I drove home that day ashamed of the role I'd played so skillfully, but feeling cautiously hopeful I might learn to be myself.

All week long I agonized. I prayed as I hadn't prayed in months: *God, what if I tell them who I really am? What if they know I'm terrified? What if they reject me? Talk bad about me? Fire me?* I swallowed hard. Then I ventured a step further: *Is this what You want me to do?* I thought I sensed God's assurance, but I wasn't sure. Desperately I hoped it was Him leading me, and not just my own whacked-out thoughts.

The next Sunday arrived, and I walked to the platform uncharacteristically unprepared—not one written note. The only preparation was in my heart. My throat dry, nervous beyond description, I stared at two hundred very committed churchgoers. They stared politely back.

Silence.

Finally I spoke. "My relationship with God is not what it should be." My voice quavered with each syllable. No one moved. I plunged ahead. "I've confessed to God, but now I'm going to confess to you: I've become a full-time minister but a part-time follower of Christ."

You could have heard a communion wafer snap.

I continued speaking, opening my heart and inviting everyone inside. The message that Sunday was unembellished: no humor, no quotes, no poems. It was void of clever sayings or points starting with the same letter. But the message was true. I held nothing back. It was the biggest public risk I'd ever taken. It was also my first *authentic* sermon. I had preached many times before, but this was the first time the real me made a showing. In the middle of my talk, something started to happen, something new…

God made Himself known.

The reality of His presence is hard to describe, but it's even harder to miss. Some people cried quietly in their seats. Others sobbed openly—not so much for my sins, but for their own. Before I had finished my confession, many gathered at the altar to repent along with me.

As the tears and words flowed, God's peace replaced my fear. His assurance pushed away my doubts. Christ's power invaded my weakness. In that moment, Jesus became as real to me as He had ever been. The Savior was with me…and I believed He was pleased. "Well done," I felt, more than heard.

That's when it all changed. I became a full-time follower of Christ who happened to be a pastor. No more make-believe. No posing. And no playing games. From that moment on, I would be who I am.

Or nothing at all.

LEAP OF FAITH

Why would you want to read a book about a pastor's confessions? Maybe you don't. But then again, maybe if you give

Him a chance, God will do something in you that you didn't expect. Like He did for me.

Be honest with yourself. Are you tired of pretending? Living to please others? Acting a part? Doing everything to cover up who you really are? Stop hiding.

Be who God called you to be. Live for an audience of ONE.

Am I saying you have to confess all your garbage in front of a whole church? No. With some issues, that might be what God requires of you. But with more personal matters, it'll be wiser to divulge them only to a small, trusted circle of friends or a lone accountability partner. But playing the fugitive from truth will never bring you peace.

The problem is that it's easier to stay the way you are—to coast and live an average, complacent life. You could avoid risk and keep acting. That's what most people do. In fact, you'll often be rewarded for faking it. No one will complain. The status quo is always comfortable. You'll blend in. Even though you know you were created to stand out.

But if you're sick of shallow, empty relationships—if you're craving deep, sincere community—then you're going to have to take a chance. You'll risk harsh judgments, mis-understandings, criticism. But think about the reward. Imagine living in the freedom and holiness of God. Dream about releasing guilt, shame, fear, and doubts. See yourself closer to God—and the people around you—than you've ever been before.

The choice is yours: Life as it has been, or life as it could become.

It is my goal to live the most authentic, transparent, vulnerable life a Christ follower can. And here is what I've found: Some people don't like me. But that would be the case no matter what, wouldn't it? On the other hand, others not only like me, they love me deeply. And they don't love the image I once portrayed. They love the *real* me who God created. And I love them.

The more honest I have become with God, myself, and His people, the richer and deeper my relationships have grown. Before, I was always afraid of being found out. I lived in constant fear of exposure—but not anymore. I overcame my fear because I took a chance. And I'll continue to take obedient, truthful chances.

This book is all about risks. As you turn each page, you'll likely experience new discomforts. This road of honesty is the path I chose to take. I won't play it safe. And neither should you. In fact, *you can't play it safe and please God*. The Bible says, "Without faith it is impossible to please God" (Hebrews 11:6).

Even when our faith is small, God can do great things. I pray that my confessions will help you take that first step toward living a life free of fear…and secrets…and doubts… and insecurities. A life of honesty. A life that pleases God. The life you were created to live.

I Can't Stand a Lot of Christians

I love Christ. It's His followers who make me crazy.

Truth is, I dislike a lot of Christians. Notice I didn't say *some* Christians, but *a lot* of them. I don't like them—not at all, not even a little bit. Many times I'd rather hang around wild, swearing, heathen, lost people than self-righteous, hypercritical, narrow-minded, so-called believers.

I relate a lot to a certain pastor of a large church. He once told a reporter in an interview that he prays for six hours a day. Astonished, the reporter asked why he prays so long. The pastor replied honestly, "My church is very large—and there are so many people that I hate—I have to pray six hours to help me love them."

I wish I liked all Christians, but I don't. Here's the short list of reasons why. I dislike many Christians because they can be so darned judgmental. They act holier-than-thou, and they can be incredibly condescending. They'll fight and argue about the dumbest things.

You're reading the wrong Bible version.

Your church has the wrong worship style.

You don't teach enough from the Old Testament.

Why don't you do more expository preaching?

Your church isn't evangelistic enough.

You are too evangelistic, and you don't do enough discipleship.

These "church experts" are often the ones who don't know their own lost next-door neighbor's name! Aaauuuggghhhh! It makes me sick. Then when you get outside of church issues, it's even more fun:

All R-rated movies are off-limits. (I loved it when *The Passion of the Christ* came out.)

If you listen to secular music, you're of the devil.

Don't get a tattoo.

Don't watch Teletubbies.

Don't go to Disney World.

I can't picture Jesus drawing these lines in the sand.

Another guy who turns my stomach is Angry Street Preacher: *Turn or burn! You're going to hell, you sinner!* In my own experience, Angry Street Preacher is often sinning as much as or more than any of the passersby he's shouting at.

If my previous rant wasn't enough, to top it off, Christians can be just plain weird—*really* weird. Take Christian television. Some of those people make my job almost impossible. If even

I—supposedly on the same team with them—am tempted to make fun of their goofiness, is it any wonder that non-Christians watch them just for laughs? I know some very valuable Christian ministries are on television, and I'm all for them, but you have to admit, there's some out-and-out flaky stuff.

If you're offended, be honest for a moment. Have you seen the way many of the televangelists dress? Add to it their overly made-up wives' long eyelashes and Pepto-Bismol-colored hair. They look like a pimp and his bimbo—and even the real pimp and the real bimbo would call it bad taste. Not to mention the unbiblical, self-centered, God-is-going-to-make-me-rich-so-I-can-drive-a-Rolls-Royce crap.

Then they top it off with that phony, insincere, I'm-going-to-get-your-money way of preaching, adding an "-uh!" to the end of every sentence. "And…Jesus rose from the grave-uh! And He will forgive your sins-uh! Call on Him now-uh!"

WHAT'S THAT?

It makes me want to puke-uh!

Probably the worst, though, is that Christians can be so stinking hypocritical. They'll say one thing and do another. Not only does that tarnish Jesus' name, but it gives the skeptical, nonbelieving world more ammunition to use against the body of Christ.

It's like the guy who went to the Baptist pastor and said, "Brother Smith, would you perform a funeral for my dead dog?"

Brother Smith replied, "We don't do funerals for dogs."

"Oh," the man replied, seeming disappointed, but inwardly smiling. "I was going to give $100,000 to the church. I guess I'll have to give it to the Methodists."

"Wait a minute!" Brother Smith quickly replied. "Why didn't you *say* your dog was a Baptist?"

Those are a few of the reasons I dislike a lot of Christians. To be fair, a lot of them don't like me, either. I'm too radical. I have shallow theology. I'm too good at marketing. And my unpardonable sin: I pastor a "megachurch" (which automatically makes me an egomaniac who only cares about money).

Now that that's on the table, we can start, and hopefully we can get somewhere God wants us to be—which is probably not where I am right now. Just the same, I feel better after venting.

Thanks for listening.

THE CHRISTIAN I DISLIKE THE MOST

If you think I only dislike Christians from other churches, think again. As I look at my own church, I see a lot of people I also don't like. I despise what they stand for and how they live. It embarrasses me—makes me sick.

One Christian stands out in my mind as the absolute worst. This guy bothers me the most. Keeps me up at night. Makes my stomach churn. The Christian I detest the most is…

Me.

I'm not kidding. I hate so much about myself. I hate when I'm less than Christ would want me to be. I despise myself when I say things I shouldn't say and things that are inconsistent with God's Word. I hate when, as a leader, I make decisions that hurt people. I hate when my sinful actions hurt Christ followers and turn away nonbelievers. With everything in me, I hate these things about myself.

My wife would chime in here and say, "Craig, you're being way too hard on yourself." She'd be right. Yes, I'm growing, and part of my growth is learning to accept myself as Christ accepts me—but I can accept myself while still hating my screwups. Those still happen way too often.

I don't like a lot of Christians—and my name often tops that list. But while I despise my own sinful actions the most, it's so much easier to point my finger at others. When I take a gut-honest look at this contradiction inside me, it shows me exactly what I need to do about it. Instead of following my instinctive course of self-defense and outward criticism, I here and now commit to laying my heart bare before God. I ask Him to cleanse *me*. Change *me*. Work in *me*.

Rather than complaining about inconsequential little irritations, I'm asking God to get right to the root of the problem, to eradicate the dry rot and fix the cracks in my foundation. I need Him to show me how to love Him and how to love His people. Even the ones I don't like—even myself.

God, make me different.

That's exactly what He's doing. Through the rest of this chapter, I'll show you how God is renovating me from the inside out. I challenge you to come along with me, not just saying, "Yeah, Groeschel, you really need to change," but telling yourself, "I need to change, too."

I'm still a beginner at this, but I'm slowly getting better. I've discovered a surprising bonus that comes with letting God change me: As God continues to stretch me, I'm learning to like—or at least tolerate—other Christians who I used to hate! When God changes me, He also changes the way I see others. (I can even watch a whole program on BPC—the Bad Preaching Channel—without throwing something at the TV.)

Let's examine some areas in our lives that God wants to make different...

DIFFERENT? PROVE IT!

We must become different in our *actions*.

First Peter 1:14–15 says, "Do not conform to the evil desires you had when you lived in ignorance. But just as he who called you is holy, so be holy in all you do." So, instead of wearing the "sin police" badge, looking for faults in others, my full-time job should be submitting to the Spirit's work in my own life—becoming *holy*.

That sounds awfully intimidating to me, so let's talk about "holy." What does that mean? I'll give you a hint: It has nothing to do with your threadbare socks. In the Bible, the English word "holy" comes from the Greek and Hebrew words that mean "sacred," "consecrated," or "set apart for a special purpose." If a thing or a person is "set apart" from anything that might contaminate it, it's also "pure," another implication of holiness.

As I love God and surrender all my heart to Him, His Spirit makes me pure, different, set apart from the darkness of this world. Unfortunately, if "holy" means "set apart," the scary truth is…I don't always behave that differently from nonbelievers. Do you?

Examine your life honestly, without pretense. Don't play games. In the way you behave, are you sincerely different from your nonbelieving neighbors? Or the people at your office? Are you different in your attitudes? Your parenting? How you handle money? Is your marriage different? Are your friendships? Your morals?

If you can honestly say *yes*, then congratulations. Some Christians do live mostly holy lives. But most Christians would have to say, *I am not different enough. I'm not living purely, empowered by Christ. I'm very much like the rest of the world.*

How can I make such a bold and sweeping statement? It's not just based on my opinions. It's also supported by the well-respected research of pollster George Barna. Barna did a study[1] to discover just how different Christians are from non-Christians. His research was much more extensive than the small sampling of findings I'll share, but here are a few of his discoveries:

The first has to do with serving. Who serves more—Christians or non-Christians? If you guessed that Christians are more likely to volunteer their time to help others (including serving at their local church), you're right. Twenty-seven percent of non-Christians give their time to nonprofit causes in an average month, compared with 29 percent of believers. Christians outshined nonbelievers in serving by a whopping 2 percent! Not exactly a convincing difference.

How about donating to charitable groups? Christians are surely much more generous, right? Actually, wrong. Forty-eight percent of non-Christians said they gave in the last month, compared to only 47 percent of Christians.

Did you catch that? Non-Christians are more generous than believers! Let's stop for a moment. What else does that staggering statistic tell us? If 47 percent of believers gave, that means 53 percent didn't. *Over half of American Christ followers didn't give any money to missions, to their church, or to the poor.* This is a colossal tragedy.

Shall we continue?

Did you know that in the year the study was conducted, 10 percent more non-Christians gave to the poor than did believers? Shocking. Did you know that exactly the same proportion of believers as nonbelievers (36 percent) read their horoscopes? (Oh, you're a Leo? It's a great day to fall in love or buy a goldfish.)

Get this one: Twenty-seven percent of born-again adults have been divorced, compared to 23 percent of non-born-again adults. It seems that more people who promised *God* not to get divorced ended their marriages than those married by the justice of the peace.

God calls us to be different. Sometimes we are...in the wrong ways.

God, make us different in our actions.

MORE THAN A HINT AT THE MALL

When I ask God to change *my* actions, that honesty about my own inconsistent behaviors forces me not to be so hard on other believers. Humble acknowledgement of the plank in my own eye gives me more patience with the specks in everyone else's (see Matthew 7:1–5). Instead of pointing the finger at others, let's allow God to examine us.

Measure your actions in light of Scripture. "Among you there must not be *even a hint of sexual immorality*, or of any kind of *impurity*, or of *greed*, because these are improper for God's holy people. Nor should there be *obscenity, foolish talk* or *coarse joking*" (Ephesians 5:3–4, emphasis mine).

Ask yourself: *In the past week, did I have even a hint of sexual*

25

immorality? *Did I think an impure thought, read something inappropriate?* (You might be surprised what God would call inappropriate.) *Did I look longingly at an attractive person who is not my spouse? Or much worse? Did I experience any kind of impurity? Greed? Obscenity? Foolish talk? Coarse joking?* God calls you to be holy, different, set apart, pure. Are you?

I had an unusual experience at the mall. I circled the lot several times, unwilling to settle for a bad parking space. As my family grew impatient, suddenly the Lord provided!

The space was very close to the best mall entrance. Driving the correct direction down the lane (and enjoying my sense of moral superiority over those who didn't), I made "eye-lock" with the Chosen Spot. If you don't know what eye-lock is, it's similar to calling "shotgun." By staring at the parking space without looking away, I created an invisible force field around it. I wrapped it in imaginary yellow tape with the word "MINE" printed boldly on it over and over. The parking space was set apart for me: "Holy unto Craig."

Now, when Person A makes eye-lock on a parking spot, it's a major breach of ethics for Persons B, C, D, E, or F to take that spot. (If I were writing the laws, it would be a crime punishable by jail time.)

Just as I pulled up, a small sports car whipped up (driving the wrong way down the lane), broke through my eye-lock force field, and *stole my space.*

I snapped. I backed up my oversized, gas-guzzling SUV (capacity eight), pointed it toward the enemy's sports car, shifted to neutral, and revved my engine: *Vrrroooom. Vrrroooom.* Then I shifted to drive, floored it, and sped directly toward his bumper.

My kids prayed aloud. My wife screamed. A split second before impact, I slammed on the brakes, screeching to a halt inches away from the other car's bumper. Then I just stared hatefully in the other driver's direction: Pastor Craig at his best.

Eventually I calmed down. I parked in an incredibly bad spot and walked into the mall with my family. Inside JCPenney, the driver of the sports car spotted me. I could tell he was sincere when he said, "Man, I'm sorry I took your spot." My wife giggled behind me.

I pondered educating him about his breach of etiquette, pontificating eloquently on the evil. I wanted to expound on the eternal consequences of shattering the eye-lock force field. He looked at me earnestly and said calmly, "It looks like you have a problem with anger. Did you know Jesus loves you?" He next proceeded to witness to me sweetly.

Did I mention that I hate the way I act?

God, make my actions different. Help me be set apart, pure, holy.

And as God makes me more like Christ, it's amazing how much more I'm willing to accept and love His flawed followers—including myself.

ME FIRST

My parking-lot debacle brings up another way I need to change. Not only do my actions need the cleansing power of the Spirit of God, but so do my *attitudes*. I tend to accuse others, while at the same time excusing myself. If someone does something remotely wrong, I'm quick to point the finger, but if *I* do something wrong, I'm quick to justify. While I judge someone else by their actions, I judge myself by my intentions.

That's wrong.

Paul said in Philippians 2:5 that my "attitude should be the same as that of Christ Jesus." And just what *is* that attitude? "Do nothing out of selfish ambition or vain conceit, but in humility consider others better than yourselves. Each of you should look not only to your own interests, but also to the interests of others" (vv. 3–4). Notice that this passage tells us to do *nothing* out of selfish ambition—nothing. Zero. Zilch. Nada.

Yet, most of what I do is motivated by selfish ambition.

What am I gonna get out of this? What's in it for me? Will it be fun? Will I gain something? If not, count me out.

God raises the bar: I should put the interests of others ahead of my own. Easier said than done.

God, change my attitude about others.

I have a few really good friends. These great men of God would all probably take a bullet for me. One in particular is my accountability partner and close friend. John has stood by me for years. Our friendship is as good as they get.

One day we were looking at a home he was considering purchasing. We walked around the house to examine the backyard. Suddenly two man-eating dogs—a large Doberman and a ferocious Chow—charged right toward us.

Thinking only of my own safety, I pushed off from my longtime friend to gain momentum in the other direction. The unintended consequence was that I also pushed him directly toward the attacking dogs. He fell over. I ran to safety. (Some obscure, primal instinct—which fortunately only emerges in response to large doses of adrenaline—realized that I couldn't outrun the dogs...but if I outran my buddy, I'd be fine.)

Thankfully, a fence separated the dogs from us. Still, I had to deal with the reality of my actions—I had put my own safety ahead of my buddy's. To save my rear end, I pushed him toward potential disaster. John still harasses me about it.

Although I'd never intentionally harm someone, my nature is dangerously selfish and self-centered, and my self-focus can harm others just as easily as if I had acted with deliberate malice.

God, help me to put others ahead of myself. Change my attitude.

ONE OF THESE THINGS IS NOT LIKE THE OTHER

What about you? Do you care about others? Really care?

It's easier to shoot the wounded than it is to help them heal. It's more fun to judge someone's sin than to gain understanding of the pain and confusion that lies behind it. Criticizing comes more naturally than listening, more than loving. In particular, how would you honestly evaluate your attitude toward people who don't know Christ?

God, help me to love the lost as You love them.

Personally, I think a lot of non-Christians act more Christlike than Christians. Let me give you a couple of contrasting examples:

Once, a guy in his early twenties knocked on my door to share his faith with me. Although I thought that was pretty cool, I interrupted him and told him I was already a disciple of Christ. Not knowing what I did for a living, he asked me where I went to church. When I told him, he confided in me that his pastor warned him not to go to *that* church…because the pastor didn't preach the truth.

Ouch.

Now I certainly don't believe our church is right for everyone, but it would be nice if Christians didn't tear each other down. That other pastor's never met me, nor has he been to our church, yet he criticizes me openly.

Contrast him with Anthony…a waiter at one of my favorite restaurants. Every time I eat there, I always request him. He's admittedly a wild man, and he seems to be far from Christ. But he's loyal, honest, trustworthy. Most of all, Anthony is my friend.

Even though Anthony knows I'm a pastor, swearing freely around me doesn't seem to be much of an issue for him. Anthony's language is similar to what you'll hear in an episode of *The Sopranos*. F-bombs fly from his mouth without restraint—and that's just his warm-up. Honestly, I like that about him. Anthony is simply himself: no airs, no pretense, no hypocrisy. I'd rather hang out with a nonbeliever who is himself than a Christ follower putting on a show.

Anthony told me about a group of restaurant patrons who were making fun of megachurch pastors, and my name came up. Anthony almost foamed at the mouth as he recounted what he had said to them:

"Guys, you don't know Craig like I do. You're full of *#@&! You need to shut the #@!% up!"

Did I mention Anthony is my friend?

What about you? So many self-centered and self-righteous believers judge those who don't know Christ:

His profanity bothers me.

They're shacking up.

Can you believe the trashy way that wild, sinful, Jezebel-spirited floozy dresses?

If these people don't know Christ, why should they be judged by His standards? How would Jesus treat such a person? With His best love. If you find yourself looking down on those who haven't fully submitted to His grace, pray:

God, change my attitude about the lost.

RESCUE THE RESCUERS?

God, change my attitude about Your church—especially my role in it.

Something just happened that made me stop and think. I was sitting in my office, typing away, when Package Delivery Guy dropped off a package. (I know his name, but I'm guarding his anonymity.) I like this guy a lot. I see him often, and he's really cool, but he just said something that makes my skin crawl.

Package Delivery Guy told me, "I finally found me a good church." (This is after several years of church hopping and shopping.) "All the other ones didn't meet my needs, but this one does."

Why would I shudder at that statement? Think about it. I've heard it hundreds of times: *I'm looking for a church that meets my needs.*

Can you admit for a moment how incredibly unbiblical that statement is? When did we, as Christ followers, start to think that the church exists for us? When did we forget that *we are the church?* And that we're here *for the world?*

Before I was a pastor, I used to think that church should serve me, until I let God change my attitude. I was a taker, not a giver. I wanted a church that would provide what I needed. I was the spiritual consumer—an observer, not a participant.

If that's you, let me encourage you to stop observing and get in the game. Reach out. Use your gifts. Give recklessly. Serve passionately. *Make a difference.* Love those whom others reject, even those who aren't like us—*especially* those who aren't like us. Love not only nonbelievers, but also "second-class Christians." Jesus did; so should we.

One time I preached at a small country church. The volunteer receptionist told me we'd be having a guest that day. (Someone had called to find out what time the service started.) I was greeting people at the front door, and sure enough, I saw the first-time guest. She was easy to spot because her clothes were not "church clothes." This apparent single mom walked nervously toward the church, Bible in hand, obviously intimidated. Suddenly one of the deacons walked up to her and told her that her clothes were unacceptable for Sunday worship. Downcast, the woman left.

Rejected...by the very people who claim to represent Christ.

God must have been crushed, furious—probably both. Yet, how often do we see God's people acting in similar ways? Prejudice is the exact opposite of what Christ calls us to: serving others. Prejudice rejects someone because of skin color, or lack of education, or the part of town the person lives in. Prejudice discriminates based on denominational backgrounds, worship preferences, and income levels.

It *must* stop.

The church is not here for us. We *are* the church, and we are here *for the world*. When I ask church people to serve somewhere, I often receive a polite, "I'll pray about it, Pastor." (Which generally means, "Oh, crap. I don't want to do that, but I'll say something spiritual that may buy me time to plan my excuse.")

I love the story about the guy who waited patiently in line to greet his pastor one Sunday after the sermon. "Pastor," this eager, sincere Christ follower said, "I have only one thing to tell you. My answer is yes. Now, what's the question?"

The pastor looked at him, confused, and, smiling awkwardly, fell back upon the pastor's safety net: "God bless you." The pastor politely brushed the man off and turned to greet the next parishioner.

The next week, the same guy waited in line and repeated the same words. "Pastor, my answer is yes. Now what's the question?"

The pastor pondered this enigma. Wanting to get to the bottom of it, he invited the young man to lunch. Over a midweek meal, the young man once again blurted out the intriguing mantra: "Pastor, my answer is yes. Now what's the question?"

Finally overcome with curiosity, the pastor asked, "Can you please tell me what you mean by that?"

The young man smiled and, with passion, began, "Pastor, I was hooked on everything bad, about to lose my family, sliding down a slippery slope toward certain destruction. Then Jesus intervened." Tears welled up in his eyes. "Because of what Jesus did for me, my answer to you is yes. You are my pastor, and I'll do whatever you need.

"If you want me to rock babies, I'll rock babies. If you want me to usher, I'll usher. If you want me to mow the churchyard, I'll be there at 6 a.m. every Saturday. My answer to you will always be yes. Now, what's the question?"

When it comes to your church (assuming you have one), what's your answer? Is it, *I'll pray about it*, while you look for an escape? Or is it...

Yes?

LOVIN' IT!

So, enough about what I don't like about Christians (myself included). Let me tell you what I *do* like—in fact, what I *love*.

I love my weekly small-group Bible study. These are some of the best people I know. They're imperfect and they're real. The other night, one guy whom we all respect talked about his problem with lust. I admire him for that. God is changing him. I love that a lot. I love the anonymous person who brought me a tin of chocolate chip cookies—just to brighten my day. I love that people donate to Christian radio and to third-world countries, to send teenagers to camp and to help hurricane victims. I love it when Christ followers sacrifice—when they give up something they love for something they love even more.

I love when God's people pray…and when He answers. I love when people use their spiritual gifts, and when they make a difference. I love to see Christ's servants blown away by the way God's using them.

I love when people "get it"—when they start to understand God's grace, and they can't help talking about it. I love when imperfect people run up against a perfect God…and God wins.

TWO

I Have to Work Hard to Stay Sexually Pure

O uch! It's tough to admit those words to myself. It's even worse to see them written on a page, where that embarrassing admission just sits there, glaring back at me—where other people will see it, too.

I wish my story was clean. I'd like to tell you that when my wife, Amy, and I dated, we loved Jesus so much that keeping our hands to ourselves was easy...a piece of cake: no heavy make-out sessions, no wandering hands, no runaway thoughts.

That would be a lie.

I wish that when I became a pastor, all sexual temptations vanished—that God supernaturally shielded my eyes, body, and mind, that all past sinful thoughts and memories disappeared, that every temptation to glance at the wrong things faded, that my mind became like Christ's.

If only that were true.

Before we continue, you need to know that this topic makes my wife uncomfortable. Amy (who is simply amazing) would tell you she's nervous about my transparent confessions—especially those regarding sexual vulnerabilities. However, because she believes in Christ's power to set people free, she completely supports this work.

Most people avoid discussing sexual purity, especially around churches. When it *is* discussed, it's generally superficial, out of touch, and watered-down, or it's the other extreme—the heavy-handed, sex-is-bad-and-only-for-procreation-so-whatever-you-do-DON'T-enjoy-it message.

Not here. Truth, authenticity, transparency, and hope-filled grace are my goals.

And speaking of truth, I must admit that I am, for better or worse, writing this chapter from a guy's perspective. The male experience is what I know, so I'll mostly deal with that. But don't ever think that sexual purity is only a male issue. Women have to work hard to avoid temptation, too. You'll just have to forgive me if I don't talk about the ladies' side quite as much.

Okay, I'm going to type fast and get the truth out, blunt and to the point, without holding back. Some of what you read may embarrass you. Parts may make you smile. But if you're honest, as I will be, you may find you identify with much of my story.

SEXUALLY CURIOUS KID

My childhood was characterized by intense curiosity about the opposite sex. You know, innocent (or not-so-innocent) inquisitiveness. Most kids have it.

For a few years, I settled for casual observations of the differences between boys and girls. One day, the pressure just became too much. With unbridled passion, I stripped the clothes off my sister's Barbie Doll. Barbie was buck naked… and I liked it. I'd seen my first naked woman. The fact that she was plastic made no difference to me.

I discovered nude pygmies in a mid-1970s issue of *National Geographic* magazine and stared contentedly at them. My friends joined me. We'd laugh, tell jokes, feel guilty…and then look some more.

That was just the beginning.

Some families had cable television with R-rated movie channels. Mine didn't—but we had the fuzzy channel. Although the TV signal was encrypted and the images were blurred, I discovered that if you watched long enough, you could occasionally see something that looked like a naked grownup…doing grownup sexual things. Then it would quickly become fuzzy again. I loved the fuzzy channel.

Up to this point, my experiences were pretty innocent compared to many young children today. Naked Barbies are the least of our worries. Because of the Internet, kids have easier access to more porn than ever before. In a recent study, nine out of ten children between the ages of eight and sixteen said they had seen porn online. And most of them said they stumbled upon it accidentally while doing their homework.[2] My relative naïveté remained intact until I was ten—when my first exposure to out-and-out porn shattered it. My childhood friend, Stephen, also ten, was my supplier. Or maybe I should say Stephen's dad was the unwitting purveyor for both of us. Stephen had discovered his dad's hidden stash of *Playboy* magazines. My lucky friend beamed when he boasted his discovery to me. Together we inspected those pages in total awe.

I clearly remember the adrenaline rush driving the turn of each page. I didn't know what it was like to do drugs, but it must have felt similar to the hormone-charged thrill of looking at these off-limits pictures.

I remembered the pictures vividly—as if they were burned onto the hard drive of my brain. Years later, I could still recall exactly what I'd seen. I couldn't always remember to do my homework, but I could retrieve Miss February's image in an instant.

It didn't help preserve what shreds of sexual innocence remained when, at the prepubescent age of twelve, I was introduced to the idea of masturbation by—believe it or not—the teacher of a church sex-education class. According to her logic, relieving the tension of this God-given impulse would keep us from doing something worse.

My parents were furious.

Armed with "revelations" from porn, sporadic parental advice, encouragement to masturbate, and many ideas from my friends (most of which I later discovered were not true), I ventured into the world of high school: car dates, proms, short skirts, truth or dare, beer…and bad movies. All were the makings of a very dangerous time.

The slippery slope of sin became steeper and more slippery every week. First, I made out with a girl. Then I went to second base. Third. Before long, I'd given away my virginity.

I knew I'd never get it back.

FROM CASANOVA TO CHRISTIAN

For a season, I pursued selfish, sinful sexual satisfaction. I'll spare you the details…but it got ugly fast.

By the time I was a sophomore in college, I was dragging around heavy chains of sin. My image—and not my will—drove all my decisions. I was trapped in daily-woven webs of deceit.

Desperate, I reached out to God for freedom.

He didn't waste any time, and He didn't skimp on His life-changing power. One ordinary day, I was walking across the college campus to class. An older man who was a member of The Gideons—an organization whose Bibles you've seen in motel and hospital rooms—was handing out free New

Testament Bibles. Spotting me—and maybe sensing the fear and pain welling up inside me—he said warmly, "You look like you could use one of these." Was he ever right.

For the first time in my life, I started reading the Bible. I devoured it. I couldn't get enough. As I began pursuing God, He was pursuing me. Finally on one fantastic day, I surrendered all to Him…or so I thought.

My life changed immediately. The reality of the risen Christ—His love and grace—quickly filled my heart. In a single moment, I was transformed. Saved. Forgiven. And very different. My party friends said I "got religion." This phenomenon was the talk of my small college, on par with a mass UFO sighting. The wildest hell-raiser on campus had become a Bible-thumper, a Jesus freak, a fanatic. Overnight, God dominated every area of my life, except one.

I still wanted to have sex.

Truthfully, it had become a part of my life. To say I "wanted it" is really an understatement. At the time, I believed I needed it. I didn't know how to let it go—or even if I really wanted to. But I knew the fight for purity was one I *had* to win.

So, finally, after a lot of battling with myself and my sinfulness, I surrendered, completely, 100 percent. I prayed sincerely, "God, I won't fulfill my selfish, lustful desires. I promise I'll live a sexually pure life."

One short prayer, one tough road ahead.

LIKE A VIRGIN

Although that road was filled with potholes and broken glass, it was also marked by a series of greater and greater victories.

For two years, I completely stopped dating. People thought I was out of my mind, but I was obeying what I believed God had shown me. The next girl I dated, I married.

Although we weren't perfectly pure while dating, Amy and I waited until our honeymoon to share the gift of lovemaking. This decision became a blessing that no one can ever take from us.

On our honeymoon night, I prepared a bowl of water. Imitating Jesus, I knelt and washed my bride's feet, explaining that I would serve her as Christ served His church. We read the Bible together. We prayed with passion. Then I unwrapped my wedding gift, and we shared in the holy, right, and pure gift of married lovemaking. Sealing our covenant vows was one of the most spiritual moments of my life. For me, it was confirmation of God's healing miracle. I experienced sex as though I'd been reborn as a brand-new virgin.

Married at last, I assumed all the sexual temptations I once battled would vanish.

How wrong I was.

FLIRTING WITH DANGER

I was a newlywed and an associate pastor, and no one I knew talked about sexual temptation. I kept my thoughts and struggles to myself. Most people do.

Plenty of guys would probably say that my vulnerabilities were minor and normal. I'd occasionally do a double take at a woman—a woman I wasn't married to, that is—or watch an R-rated movie with lots of skin. My little indulgences weren't doing any real harm...or so I thought.

My long sleepwalk ended during one painfully sobering moment on a ministry trip. I had just finished preaching and was at the airport waiting to fly home. Before boarding the plane, I went to use the men's restroom. In the privacy of a restroom stall, I noticed a magazine on the floor next to the toilet. I leaned over to see what it was. It was a *Playboy* magazine.

Suddenly my heart raced. I felt that familiar druglike rush. There I was, all alone, an anonymous man in a private stall at an airport far from home...a *Playboy* within easy reach.

But I wasn't just any guy. I was a Christian...and I was a pastor.

I wish I could tell you I thought, *How sad. I'll pray for the poor person who bought this. I'll throw it away so no one else will be tempted.* I wish I could tell you that, but it wouldn't be true. Instead, I was seized by a sinful desire to look.

By the grace of God, I didn't. Somehow I came to my senses and escaped the trap. But I also realized just how vulnerable I was, and it scared me. What was *wrong* with me? I loved my wife. I loved Jesus…but I still *wanted* to look.

Years later I told that story in church. Many were shocked at my honesty. To my surprise, several men chuckled and said, "I would've looked," or, "Man, you're *way* too serious about purity. Looking at that stuff is no big deal."

For me, sexual purity has become a profoundly big deal. It should be for you, too. Why am I so serious about purity? Because God's serious about it. Ephesians 5:3 says, "But among you there must not be *even a hint* of sexual immorality" (emphasis mine).

Not even a hint.

What is a hint of sexual impurity? Certainly looking lustfully at someone in a magazine, on television, or in person would fall somewhere north of the "hint" mark, wouldn't it? Jesus said that just to *look* lustfully at someone is the same as committing adultery. Yet I know many people who say, "I'm just window shopping, not buying."

How's your thought life? Do you catch your mind wandering to sexually explicit thoughts about someone besides your spouse? Impurity. Laughing at that sexual joke in the break room at work? Impurity. Are you honoring God by reading women's magazines with articles like, "73 Sinful Ways to Drive Your Man Crazy in Bed"? Or by dropping sexual innuendos? Or masturbating? The list could go on and on.

You have to quit playing your little rationalization games. You know you're justifying sin. It's wrong. Worse, it's dangerous.

What if you're a single person? What should your standard of purity be? Just fooling around? You know, "doing everything but"? A quick game of naked Twister? How about a sleepover? We won't mess around. We'll just cuddle in bed. WARNING! BOUNDARY VIOLATION!

Why are those things wrong? Because they're intimate acts reserved for marriage. Sex. Undoing bras or zippers. Messin' around. All these are appropriate for marriage...but none are appropriate outside of marriage.

I have performed wedding ceremonies for three couples who saved their first *kiss* for their wedding day. Why? Because they saw kissing as an intimate act reserved for marriage. Now *that's* a commitment to purity.

Not even a hint.

For me, sexual purity is vital. Why? Because the stakes are so high. If I fell into sexual sin, I would break God's heart and drag His name through the mud. When I met my heavenly Father face-to-face, I'd have to answer for those sinful actions. I would lose my wife's trust and inflict untold hurt upon her. I'd risk losing my family and the admiration and respect of my children. I'd lose my reputation and my job as a pastor. Everything that matters to me could be destroyed in a moment.

The same is true for you.

THE BEST DEFENSE

I've been very honest about my struggles. Now allow me to speak honestly about my successes. I've lived for several years at a level of sexual purity I didn't even believe was possible. Don't get me wrong: I'm still tempted…just as you will always be. Remember, it's not a sin to be tempted…it's *how you respond* to temptation that matters.

My thought life is purer than it's ever been. My sex life with my wife is holy and gratifying. Christ has made me strong where I was weak. Not for a moment do I believe that I've arrived, but God has given me some proven biblical principles that absolutely work. They're not easy to live by, but they're effective. I want to share with you the lessons I've learned on the hard road to purity.

King David was a man with a heart for God—and yet he stumbled. His life reveals several hazards to watch for on the dangerous road of life. Here's his story:

> In the spring, at the time when kings go off to war, David sent Joab out with the king's men and the whole Israelite army.…

But David remained in Jerusalem. One evening David got up from his bed and walked around on the roof of the palace. From the roof he saw a woman bathing. The woman was very beautiful, and David sent someone to find out about her. The man said, "Isn't this Bathsheba, the daughter of Eliam and the wife of Uriah the Hittite?" Then David sent messengers to get her. She came to him, and he slept with her.... Then she went back home. The woman conceived and sent word to David, saying, "I am pregnant." (2 Samuel 11:1–5)

In five short verses, the Bible tells how David's life was turned upside down with one wrong decision. But the wisdom we gain from reading about David's sin may keep the same thing from happening to us.

READY OR NOT, TEMPTATION IS COMING

The first thing we learn from his mistake is to *watch for temptation*. Always be ready. I don't wonder *if* I'll be tempted—I try to establish action plans for the times *when* I'm tempted.

You may have noticed that David wasn't where he was supposed to be. Verse 1 says that at the time of year when kings normally went off to war, David stayed behind. Temptation has a way of finding the person who's in the wrong place. That's why the best defense is to avoid tempting situations completely.

I never travel alone. It's been years since I've been alone with a woman other than my wife. We don't have the wrong kind of movie channels, and I've asked a friend to monitor all my Internet activity. By planning ahead, I've eliminated many temptations before they start. If I didn't avoid temptation, I know that resisting it would be more difficult, and I might give in.

Maybe you find yourself beaming with confidence, thinking, *I'm strong. I don't need those kinds of precautions to keep from sinning.* Remember the warning of 1 Corinthians 10:12: "If you think you are standing firm, be careful that you don't fall!"

Are you really honest with yourself about your vulnerability, or do you live on the edge of danger? If I sound overly dramatic, it's only because I care. I've seen too many good people slide into destruction because they weren't willing to be honest.

One of these people was a mentor of mine, a pastor and close friend. I'll call him Barry. Barry and I prayed together weekly and talked openly about our weaknesses...or so I thought. Little did I know, Barry had a porn problem. His "little sins" led to bigger sins, and he ended up committing adultery. Haunted by shame and guilt, one day my good friend—father of two—hung himself.

I buried my friend. If only he'd been honest!

Sexual temptation is dangerous. What starts as a thought can lead to a look, followed by lingering thoughts, which can quickly become actions. The statistics are staggering. Conservative studies show that more than 60 percent of men and 40 percent of women commit adultery.[3] Christians aren't exempt from this danger. Watch for temptation.

The danger reminds me of a story about how Eskimos sometimes deal with predatory wolves. To protect the families in a village from harm, someone hunts down a rabbit or a squirrel. Then the villagers dip a sharp two-edged knife into the animal's blood and allow the blood to freeze on its blade. They bury the handle of the knife firmly in the ground with the blood-covered blade exposed.

During the night, a wolf inevitably smells the blood and approaches to investigate. It starts to lick the knife blade. The frozen blood and cold metal numb the wolf's tongue as he continues to lick. Eventually, he slices his own tongue on the blade, and he tastes his own warm blood. Numb to the pain, the wolf licks faster and faster and faster. Without realizing it, he slices his own tongue to shreds. By the time he knows what's happened, too much damage has been done. The wolf slowly bleeds to death.

Pretty gross story, huh? But what a vivid and accurate

analogy illustrating what happens to a person who starts dabbling in the world of sexual darkness.

No one wakes up one morning and says, "Gee, I think I'm going to destroy my life. Everything's going so great; I'm going to do something really stupid." Yet, countless people inflict just this kind of destruction on themselves...especially when it comes to sex.

Watch for temptation. Avoid it whenever possible. Recognize it when it comes. And when it does come, do what that Gump guy said: *Run, Forrest, run!*

And most of all, be honest. You may be gambling far more than you know.

JUST ONE LITTLE PEEEEEEEEEEK?

The second thing we learn from David is to *watch what we watch*. Verse 2 says, "From the roof he saw a woman bathing. The woman was very beautiful."

It's not a sin to notice a beautiful person, but it becomes a sin when you notice and notice and notice...and keep noticing. That's what David did.

The Hebrew word for "saw" is the word *ra'ah*. It implies an extended gaze with enjoyment. *In other words, he lusted.* If you notice someone attractive, you can innocently and purely think, *That's a nice-looking person.* Or you can *rrrrrraaaAA'aaaahhHHhh! Whoa! Did you see that? Hubba hubba hubba! I'd like some of that!*

You get the point.

When Amy and I first set up Internet access, we tried the free AOL thing. Before long we got some strange e-mail. We opened it and were shocked that it led to a porn site. I closed it immediately. That's when I realized I had access to instant porn, just like everyone else who uses the Internet. What used to be difficult to get is now just a click away. That's why I have all my Web activity monitored. I know I'm not perfect, so I have to be smart.

And it's not just the Internet. Sexual temptation comes in every form imaginable. One of my friends loves to *ra'ah* the Victoria's Secret catalog. Another loves to *ra'ah* the wrong shows on HBO. One church member lusts after girls at the gym. Another undresses girls in his mind, *at church.* One female friend told my wife how a sinful chat room relationship took her down. Many are sucked into sexual sin through doorways that most would call acceptable: soap operas, *Cosmopolitan,* romance novels, and *Sports Illustrated* swimsuit issues.

What are you tempted to read or watch that you know you shouldn't? Acknowledge it. You won't be free until you do. Remember God's standard? *Not even a hint.*

Watch what you watch.

POINTED ENFORCEMENT

The third thing we learn from David is to *watch our company.* Verse 4 says that "David sent messengers to get her." These messengers were probably afraid to disobey the king's orders, but a good friend would have said, "David, she's married! Don't do it! Are you nuts?"

Always remember the truth of 1 Corinthians 15:33: "Do not be misled: 'Bad company corrupts good character.'" Even good people in the wrong situation can be bad company.

If you're hanging with the wrong people, you'll end up doing the wrong things. If your friends talk about bad stuff, watch sinful movies, take you dancing at the new bar, trash-talk their spouses, or flirt with everyone they see, they'll hurt you. If one of those friends is a source of sexual temptation... you're walking right into the dragon's mouth.

Not only should we avoid the wrong company, but we also must surround ourselves with the right company. Proverbs 27:17 reminds us, "As iron sharpens iron, so one man sharpens another." Who sharpens you?

David had a friend named Nathan. Nathan became the sharpening iron—the right company—for David. He took a big risk and confronted David about his sin. David owned up and got right with God. David didn't find freedom alone. He needed the right people in his life.

So do you.

One key to sexual purity in my life is consistent, intentional accountability. This isn't a polite, occasional breakfast meeting. Real accountability partners will kick your butt if you go astray. You have to have honest talks on a rigorous schedule.

In seminary I read the writings of a medieval monk. Once, a friend of this monk committed adultery. The spiritual leader gave the order: "Find five strong monks and show this man the will of God by stripping him naked and dragging him through the thistle bushes."

Now that's accountability!

True accountability attaches consequences to sin (though they don't have to be quite as harsh as getting dragged naked through thistle bushes). My accountability partner was once battling his way to victory over a certain sexual sin. He told me that every time he failed, he'd give a hundred dollars to our church building fund. He paid for a big portion of the building. Today, he's free from that sin.

Find friends who keep you strong, not ones who bring you down.

Watch your company.

DECIDING FACTORS

The fourth warning David's life provides us is, *watch for the moment of decision*. Nine words show David's most critical moment of decision. Verse 4 says, "She came to him, and he slept with her."

Now, before his big failure, David blew through several

smaller moments of decision, committing multiple smaller sins. He wasn't where he was supposed to be. He looked lustfully. He plotted and sent someone to get Bathsheba. He flirted. He schemed…then he acted. At any point, he could've stopped and done the right thing.

You can, too.

Perhaps you've had an affair. Maybe you are having one now, or you're dangerously close. Maybe you're consistently committing adultery in your heart. Or you're addicted to masturbation or to fantasizing. Maybe you watch shows you shouldn't watch, or click on websites you know are wrong.

You can't change your past…but you can change your future.

You'll face many moments of decision: maybe a click on the computer, or dialing a sex number, or that second long look at the gym, or flirting at the office. If you decide poorly during the early, small moments, eventually you'll come to the big one. Deal with each battle one at a time. When each battle comes…*win!*

The first battle will be with yourself. If you're trapped, you have to come clean. You have to confess your sin to God and to trusted friends. James says, "Confess your sins to each other and pray for each other so that you may be healed" (James 5:16). Who do you need to confess to? Certainly to God. Maybe your spouse? Or a close friend? Or even your pastor?

Maybe you're tempted to say, "This is just the way I am—I'll never change." Quit whining, compromising, and belittling the power of Christ. Paul once wrote to a very sexually corrupt group of people: "No temptation has seized you except what is common to man. And God is faithful; he will not let you be tempted beyond what you can bear. But when you are tempted, he will also provide a way out so that you can stand up under it" (1 Corinthians 10:13).

God will give you a way out—but you have to take the first step. And the first step is to face it. Come clean.

If you're honest with yourself in this moment, and you know that breaking through to confession is the battle you now face, take just a moment...the moment of decision. Make it a victory.

What do you want to tell God? Go ahead. Tell Him right now. He's listening.

(I'll wait.)

Great! Now who else do you need to talk to? Put this book down and call them immediately.

(I'll wait, again.)

Did you call? If you're not serious, you won't beat this. You have to hate the darkness. Despise the bondage. Loathe the addiction. Make the call. *Make it now.*

(I'll go do some chores...)

Welcome back. You look relieved, peaceful. Yeah, it was scary. But isn't it nice to know you don't have to hide it anymore, that you're on your way to being free from that sin?

Remember my *Playboy*-in-the-restroom story? I felt such shame and guilt for wanting to look. Years passed. Then one day, out of the blue, I found another magazine. Again I was alone. Again it was within easy reach. This time, though, my mind was different. God had changed my heart. I loved purity more than sexual sin. What I saw made me sad, and I didn't want to look. Eyes averted, I picked up the magazine and put it in the trash. It wasn't until later that night that I realized how far God had brought me. He wants to change you, too. He *can* change you.

Not even a hint.

THREE

Most of the Time I Feel Incredibly Lonely

When God created the world, He declared that everything was good. The sun, the earth, the moon, and the stars—all good. He was pleased with the animals, pleased with the mountains, pleased with the oceans, and pleased with the trees.

Above all, God was most proud of His best work: man. All was good—except one thing. "The LORD God said, 'It is not good for the man to be alone'" (Genesis 2:18). Loneliness was the fly in God's otherwise perfect ointment—a problem He fixed by doubling the human population from one to two (and opening the way for centuries of arguments over who gets to hold the remote control).

But don't miss this important point: *God designed people*

to need each other. So, if it's not good to be alone, I have one question:

Why do I feel lonely so much of the time?

EMOTIONAL AMBUSH

Loneliness is a weird thing. If you're like me, you can stand in a crowded room and feel alone. You can have people near your person, but far from your heart. You can be the life of the party and still be relationally bankrupt.

Years ago I preached to a thousand teens at a Christian camp. On the final night, dozens of young adults pushed their way to the front to pray for salvation. Hundreds fell to their knees in humble repentance for their sins. I was awestruck by the manifestation of God's presence and stunned He would work through me in such a way.

After the service was over, I retreated to my room—alone. God had just used me powerfully to help many people, and minutes later, I felt abandoned and desperate. Dozens of people stood, sat, milled, and slept not a hundred feet from my hotel door, yet they seemed a million miles away. I was hurting and alone, and I didn't understand why.

A flood of tears took me by surprise. Then came the questions: *I'm supposed to be there for everyone else. But what happens when I hurt? When I'm afraid? Or need acceptance? Or feel* alone? *Who ministers to the minister?* One moment I was in front of a crowd, full of confidence. The next moment I was crying in the corner of a hotel room, honestly believing that no one cared whether I lived or died.

NOT ACCORDING TO PLAN

I've talked to married people aching for intimacy, kids who crave real friendships, teenagers who battle feelings of isolation. Countless single adults long for married companionship. Many older people feel abandoned, forgotten. Even leaders—you know, the ones who seem to have it all together—often feel lost in the hollowness of their souls. And God hates it. It's not good for men or women to be alone.

Why is God so passionate about loneliness? Because He deeply values relationships. He knows us better than Michelangelo knew the Sistine Chapel ceiling. So He wants us to know *Him*, and we come to know Him more by sharing His love with one another. But even though God wants people to connect intimately, many struggle with thoughts like:

No one understands me.

Does anyone genuinely care about me?

If I died, would it really matter?

No one knows the real me...and even if they did, they probably wouldn't like me.

THE POPULAR LONER

My feelings of loneliness often confuse me. You'd think a pastor would have tons of close friends. Many do. Why not me?

When I first launched into ministry, I expected my life as a pastor would come with abundant meaningful relationships. Reality ground my expectations into microscopic particles. I had visualized dozens of people ready to lend a hand at a moment's notice. I dreamed of those who would love loyally, without strings. I pictured adoring followers available to support their pastor no matter what. But those dreams quickly faded. For years, I felt as though I held slot number one on the top-ten list of loneliest people in the universe. Maybe you can relate.

Looking back, I can see that it wasn't completely the church members' fault. I needed to buck up and take responsibility for it. Sure, people placed unrealistic expectations on me—that comes with the territory. But I did the exact same thing in return. If only I had known better. I wanted friends—real friends—but I didn't know how to be one. So I pretended to have great friendships while feeling desperately alone. People were everywhere, offering me mild expressions of love: pats on the back, thank you notes. They shook my hand and said, "Nice sermon, Pastor," on their way to lunch, but not much of their kindness penetrated my heart. Why? Because, after so many disappointments, my heart had grown hard and cold.

AND FOR MY NEXT ACT...

During our first years of ministry, Amy and I sustained wounds that resulted in years of guarded living. Unconsciously, we started to withdraw our hearts from people. We didn't realize at the time that these decisions were the cause of our increasing feelings of loneliness and isolation.

I was one year out of college, making good money for a young guy in business when an aging yet strong traditional church invited me to start a Sunday school class for young adults. When attendance reached forty people, the church asked me to join the staff. That was one of the greatest days of my life. Amy and I gladly abandoned the bigger bucks for an opportunity to change lives. Instead of making money, we were going to make disciples for Christ. The lessons we learned during the next few years forever shaped our lives for the better, but it didn't always feel like we were moving forward.

As a twenty-three-year-old minister, I expected Christians to act like Christ. In case you haven't noticed, they often act more like the Antichrist. Maybe we were naïve and at times overly sensitive. Whatever the reasons, we found ourselves getting hurt by the people we thought we could trust most. Because of this, we drew a series of wrong conclusions that could have easily derailed our effectiveness for the rest of our lives.

We learned our first discouraging "lesson" within a few months of joining the staff. The young adult ministry we led began to boom. Lots of new people were finding Christ, and others were coming back to the church. First Church was growing, and for the first time in a long time, things started to change.

Before long, several of the older members began to voice alarm over the changes—especially the young people moving in on their turf. This was the kind of church where everyone had "their seat." Literally. More than once, one of the regulars relocated an unsuspecting visitor with upraised index finger and some proclamation like, "I've been sitting in this pew since 1742." Then the "rightful" owner would plop his or her pompous butt resolutely into its long-accustomed berth. (Is that what they mean by "squatter's rights"?)

The church was growing, coming alive. Some loved it. Unfortunately, many who didn't were in positions of power. One day, the head of the Big and All-Powerful Church Committee decided I needed to be fired. Six months into the job, several people wanted me gone. Welcome to the church world.

The buzzards—oops! I mean, the committee—held a meeting to decide my fate. They fought (a specialty of most committees). Several members favored my dismissal, but a few believed I represented the future of the church. In the end, the futurists won over the traditionalists...barely. The committee generously offered me one more chance.

That was when I came to my first of three dangerous conclusions:

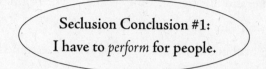

Seclusion Conclusion #1:
I have to *perform* for people.

In my case, if I didn't perform, I might not last. So I had better do a good job. Don't offend people. Say the right thing. Help the church grow, but not too much, or too fast. Don't rock the boat.

Maybe you're a performer. As a kid in school, perhaps you tried to prove your worth by making all A's. In your mind, a B was the same as an F. Maybe you strove to be the best in sports, or to make the first chair in band. As an adult, maybe you want to be the boss's favorite. Maybe you desire to become the perfect spouse or parent. So you create impossible standards for yourself and daily put on your best performance for others. The show must go on. And so does the loneliness.

AN ALTARED VIEW OF FRIENDSHIP

A second disappointment struck shortly after the first. Following each church service, we offered a time for prayer at the altar. All the pastors lined up, ready to pray with anyone who had a need. Two of my close friends approached the altar. This couple had welcomed Amy and me to their home for dinner. We talked regularly on the phone. These were friends with whom we shared our intimacies. At their request, Amy joined me, and fearing for some serious need, we prepared to pray down heaven for our friends.

The husband started nervously, "We have something to ask you." Amy and I leaned forward, ready to give our full support. The wife spoke next. "Will you forgive us?" Her voice trembled. "We've had bad thoughts about you for the last year. My husband wanted the ministry job you got, and we have despised you in our hearts. We've said bad things about you, judged you wrongly, and hoped you would lose the job."

We were stunned. Shocked. Devastated. We stared at them, not knowing what to say. How could we go a year not knowing their true feelings? How could they pretend to be our close friends, and yet hate us all that time? Things hadn't been as they seemed.

The husband apologized, prayed, and cried. He told us how much better he felt. They had carried this burden for so long. They both hugged us, then walked away feeling relieved—and left us in an emotional pool of blood.

Our insecurities drove us to ask ourselves, *Who else doesn't like us? Does anyone really care? Who can we trust?* This led to:

Seclusion Conclusion #2:
To survive in life, you
can't *trust* anyone.

Maybe you've felt the same way. To make it in this world, you always have to be on your guard. People aren't what they seem, so you must protect yourself. Don't trust them, or you will get burned. Instead, build walls and don't let anyone inside.

This faulty logic was leading me into a frigid world of isolation. I felt the chill but didn't have any clue as to the cause—me.

WHAT HOG?

We thought we were lonely before, but a few years later, another experience triggered more hurt and another wrong conclusion. Amy and I had gone three years without a pay raise. Each year, the church budget was tight, and we volunteered to leave our salary where it was. Amy stayed at home to raise our child. So, on about $1200 a month, after tithe and taxes, we were able to pay the bills, but we were by no means living an extravagant lifestyle.

When the associate pastor moved to another church, First Church "promoted" me. I took on his responsibilities while also retaining the full-time ministry to young adults. Suddenly I had two full-time jobs—but only one barely full-time salary. Then someone on the Big and All-Powerful Church Committee had an idea. I'll never forget the moment he stood and made his presentation.

"Our church has almost doubled in size," he started, "and the majority of the increase has come from our young adult ministry. Do you realize that Craig and Amy minister to three hundred people every Friday night? And now they're doing another job. I move that we give him a raise."

This time the chills I felt were good ones. Someone actually seemed to care. Now, I'm not going to tell you "it wasn't about the money," because an extra hundred dollars a month would've gone a long way. But more than the money, this man's words made us feel valued. I liked that feeling.

The committee agreed to meet to discuss our potential raise. But my balloon began to deflate before we had even walked out the door. A different member of the Big and All-Powerful Church Committee pulled me aside. With a growl and a scowl, he told me his twentysomething kids didn't make much, and he certainly wouldn't have a pastor's family living "high on the hog." (I'm just guessing, but I suspect he was planning to vote against my pay increase.)

He wasn't alone. The committee kiboshed our raise. We felt unappreciated and rejected, which led us to:

Seclusion Conclusion #3:
People don't really *care* about us.

Have you ever felt like that? People only want what's good for them. Your well-being is meaningless to anyone else.

They'll tell you they love you or that they're praying for you, but it's all show. People don't really care.

We allowed this third and dangerously wrong conclusion to harden our hearts still further and to drive us further away from relationships that could have renewed our faith in the goodness of others.

WHERE THE SUN DON'T SHINE

Speaking of driving...

We live on a few acres in the country. (I really am staying on topic. You'll see.) Country adventures are so much fun. We battle raccoons, see wild turkeys, feed deer, shoot poisonous snakes, and catch turtles. My kids love the turtles.

When we see one of our little shelled friends in the middle of a country road, the kids often want to stop and help the turtle across, so it won't get smashed by a car. (Everyone knows you can't make good soup out of roadkill in a shell.)

Whenever I drive by a turtle, I have to chuckle at his "survival instinct." There he is, his bony little head poking out on that long, skinny neck. Then when he sees my car approaching, he pulls in his limbs and head. I can't help wondering about turtle psychology: Does the illusion of safety really give him peace of mind? Is he in there lounging back in his armchair, smoking a little cigar, reading poetry? Does he really believe the car tire ceases to exist, just because he can't see it? I suppose millions of turtles throughout history have achieved a last few seconds of peace using this strategy.

For a season, Amy and I behaved like turtles. We retreated into our shell. We wouldn't trust people, wouldn't open up, wouldn't take relational risks. We just hid inside the illusion of safety. And we didn't even get a few seconds' peace out of the deal. The turtle got off better than we did.

I have to admit that the blows to our trust were minor compared to the experiences of many people we know. They may be minor compared to yours, too. Perhaps a family member betrayed you. Maybe it was a best friend, or a Christian. Maybe someone cheated you on a business deal, or someone did physical harm to you or to someone you love. You may have grown up in a very painful home...abandoned, scarred by vicious words, physically abused. You might have enjoyed a season of innocence, a time when you trusted people and thought they were decent. Then you learned a lesson the hard way. So now you go to a church but don't really know anyone there. Or you love God but avoid church altogether, not wanting to risk the relational messes. You've started to believe no one knows the real you. Your spouse, who sleeps next to you in bed every night, might as well be in another state. And even though you're around people all the time, you feel like you live in solitary confinement. You hide in your shell, living with the illusion of safety. But in reality, you are more vulnerable than ever.

ALTERNATE ENDINGS

What do we do when we're lonely, when we're relationally dry? We crave meaningful intimacy. We're thirsty for something more, and yet afraid to risk more pain. We build our response on the wrong assumptions.

I believed that since people might not like the real me, I should conjure up a fake version—the old perform-for-people ploy. Ya know, give them my best show.

Most everyone does it at least some of the time. We try to astound people with our great marriages…that aren't that great. Or we go into debt buying things we don't need with money we don't have to impress people we don't even like. Maybe it's all about making the grade, or scoring more points, or saying the right thing. We honestly believe that if we perform well enough, people will like us.

When we front a fiction, we are destined for loneliness.

I embraced the role of "the perfect pastor." Always armed with a fake smile, I'd be the first on the scene at any church event. Whatever needed doing, I made sure I was involved. I wanted everyone to recognize my superior commitment and dedication to God. At the age of twenty-six, I was performing at my peak. Not only was I carrying fifteen hours of seminary class work, but I was working a solid fifty hours a week. In my twisted thinking, I saw this lifestyle as fertile ground for my abilities to blossom. I didn't know that I was killing off virtually every relationship I had. Dying on the inside, I charged on.

One day I read Galatians 1:10. The words shook my staged world. Paul wrote, "Am I now trying to win the approval of men, or of God? Or am I trying to please men? If I were still trying to please men, I would not be a servant of Christ." Beyond a shadow of a doubt, I was trying to please the wrong audience. God slowly started to break through my stubborn performance mentality. He steered me away from living for others and gently called me back toward living for an audience of One. He showed me that I needed to surrender my life to Him and Him alone.

If you're a performer, embrace the truth that God loves and cares for you, no matter what kind of external show you put on. You can't do anything to make Him love you more— and you can't do anything to make Him love you less. You certainly shouldn't perform for people, but in an important sense, neither do you perform for God. You don't behave correctly to earn His acceptance. Instead, you live empowered by God's Spirit with the goal to please Him alone, *because He has already accepted you.* You're not who others say you are. You're who God says you are. Stop performing for others. God's opinion of you is the only one that matters. God created you, and He knows you and loves you. Your life belongs to Him, so allow Him to guide every move you make.

MUST JUST TRUST

In my quest for self-protection, the second wrong assumption I made was that I couldn't really trust people. Maybe you feel that way. Perhaps you've been burned, rejected, betrayed, or crushed. Maybe you gave someone chance after chance after chance, only to be let down again. Each time you hoped things would be different, and each time someone disappointed you more, confirming the wisdom of distrust.

The walls are up, and you're cut off, alone. You may not even realize you need a breakthrough. I can relate, because my walls were strong and high. My heart had "NO TRESPASSING" signs posted all over it. I would show others just enough of me to give an illusion of friendship, but not enough to make my heart vulnerable again. Slowly, God started to reveal to me my true need for deeper relationships. To grab my attention, He used one of my greatest fears—the fear of rejection.

I had one friend who I allowed to get "sort of" close. His name is John, and we had worked out together for a couple of years. He was very open with me and expected the same in return. I simply didn't reciprocate. I thought I had him fooled, but he shocked me one day with a bold confrontation. In the middle of our afternoon workout, he stopped lifting weights, looked me in the eyes, and said, "I thought we were becoming friends, but it's obvious we're not, and I don't have the time to hang around someone who won't be himself." Then he calmly walked out of the gym, got into his car, and drove away.

I felt more alone at that moment than I had felt in years. It was then I remembered the words my mom had told me a million times: "Son, to have a friend, you have to be a friend." In my desire to protect my heart from more hurt, I had forgotten how to be a friend. It was time to learn to trust…again.

What better example of friendship can we find in the Bible than David and Jonathan? The young shepherd David had been anointed as the next king of Israel, and the current king, Saul, was not the least bit happy about it. Consumed with jealousy, he set out to take David's life.

Then God sent David an interesting ally. It was none other than King Saul's son, Jonathan, heir apparent to the throne. If I had been David, I would have hesitated before trusting the son of my would-be assassin, but not David. First Samuel 23:16–17 records a powerful moment between these two young men: "And Saul's son Jonathan went to David at Horesh and helped him find strength in God. 'Don't be afraid,' he said. 'My father Saul will not lay a hand on you. You will be king over Israel, and I will be second to you.'" Jonathan had every reason to be jealous of David or to make his own attempt at the throne. But instead, he humbled himself to serve his friend.

Jonathan did some amazing things. First, he helped David

find strength in God. David couldn't have become the hero of later decades without his friend's support at this important stage. Second, Jonathan vowed his loyalty to protect David. And third, Jonathan put David ahead of himself. In word and action, Jonathan showed David he would bow to him in faithful service.

Remember, David had been burned by King Saul. The king had tried to run David through with a spear, among other attempts on his life. So David had every reason not to trust anyone, and yet he trusted Jonathan.

After my sobering workout conversation, I went to John, and I took one of the biggest risks in my life. I decided to trust him. "Let me tell you why I've been guarded," I started, wanting even then to back away from revealing the truth, but I plowed ahead. "As a minister, I don't know who I can trust." Then I recounted years of hurt and rejection. The words flowed. Tears welled up in my eyes. Within moments, I had vomited up years of hidden pain.

He stared at me blankly. My mind raced. *He's a layperson. He'll never understand a minister's struggles. I just blew it. He'll tell everyone what I just said. How stupid could I be?* Then a smile slowly spread across his face, and he said, "Now we're getting somewhere." I saw unconditional acceptance in his eyes, and I sensed that finally I had allowed a David-and-Jonathan friendship to become possible in my life. But that opportunity would die if I ever stopped taking the risk to trust.

So trust I did. Eleven years later, John is still my primary accountability partner. Daily he's helped me find strength in God. He's stood in the background, willing to play an anonymous role as a supportive friend, watching as God works through me in public. Someone said that if you're lonely at the top, it's because you didn't take anyone with you. They were so right.

HOW MUCH CARE CAN YOU BEAR?

My friendship with John led to others. As my frozen heart began to thaw, I started to let others in. As my circle of real friends grew, my third faulty conclusion was proven false: I had assumed that people didn't really care. I couldn't have been more wrong.

As a minister, it's my job to minister to others. Honestly, it comes naturally to me, but I'm not good at receiving ministry from others. Can you relate? It was right at the bull's-eye of this shortcoming that God aimed His next lesson for me. With four small children, my wife Amy was forced into bed rest during her fifth pregnancy. As hard as I tried, I simply couldn't handle all the responsibilities. (I harbor no illusions about my wife's job as a mother and housewife. It's infinitely more difficult than mine.)

Several days into this new arrangement, I started to panic. My thoughts drifted again to my false conclusion: *No* one really cares about us. How come I'm always there for everyone else, but no one is here for us? Then a Scripture came to mind. James 4:2 tells us that we don't have because we don't ask (my paraphrase). It dawned on me that my pride was my biggest barrier to accepting care from others.

Finally, I humbly asked for help. When I did, people came from every zip code within fifty miles and showered our family with more love and generosity than I could describe. We didn't have to make a meal for three months. People cleaned our house, mowed our lawn, planted flowers in our yard, took care of the kids, and in a variety of other ways, spoiled us rotten. Not only did people care, but they cared a lot! My pride had been the barrier.

What about you? Do you find it easier to give than to receive? Maybe your pride is blocking you from receiving great blessings from God through His people. If you battle loneliness, as my wife and I did for years, it's not going to "just go away." Instead of blaming others, look at yourself and be honest—really honest. Are you willing to risk getting hurt in order to find truly meaningful, fulfilling relationships? Are you giving and receiving the love of Christ?

If not, I dare you to do something about it.

FOUR

I Hate Prayer Meetings

The first time I prayed out loud in front of people was during my junior year in high school. Some of my friends told me that cute girls frequented the weekly Fellowship of Christian Athletes meeting.

I was in.

My buddies and I got to the FCA meeting fashionably late. We strolled into the gymnasium and casually surveyed the scenery. Sure enough, there were some good-looking girls. *Praise the Lord!*

The FCA sponsor was a coach who recognized me and shouted across the gym, "Groeschel! I didn't know you were a Christian!" (I attended church occasionally but was not a follower of Christ). "Welcome to FCA." He acted genuinely glad to see me. Taking me aside, he asked enthusiastically, "Would you say the opening prayer?"

I'd say this came out of left field, but even left field didn't see this one coming. One minute everything was normal; the next moment I was asked to pray...in public. *Yikes!* (That's actually the cleaned-up version of what I thought—my editor wouldn't let me use the original.) Speaking in public was bad enough. Praying was my worst nightmare.

Politely, I tried to decline, but he wouldn't take no for an answer. Under more pressure, reluctantly, I agreed to pray.

"Everyone, gather up!" the coach shouted.

To the expectant gathering, he explained, "Before our Bible study, I've invited Craig Groeschel to say the opening prayer." Panic set in. What was I going to say? What would people think? I knew how to pray privately—well, sort of—but praying out loud? That was for pastors.

After a long, awkward moment, I started: "Dear God..." My voice was shaking. "Thank you for this beautiful day." Then I remembered that the day was cold and dreary, not beautiful. I was crashing before takeoff. "Help us to have fun tonight." I thought everyone could hear my heart pounding. Then the inspiration struck: *Lighten it up!* Confidence swelling, I prayed, "And, God, help all the guys find dates with hot girls at FCA. Amen."

When I opened my eyes, no one was smiling.

PITIFUL IN PUBLIC

Four years later, I became a follower of Christ. I felt slightly more comfortable praying, but only when no one else was listening. To me, prayer was a private thing. During college, I had a roommate named Todd, and Todd loved to pray…and pray…and pray.

Todd especially loved to pray out loud. And for Todd, the longer the prayers, the better.

Several nights a week, Todd would invite people over for his infamously long prayer meetings. Everyone who *really* loved God would come. I loved God, but I despised these prayer meetings. We would sit in a circle and pray. *For hours.* I hate to admit it, but I got bored—really bored. My mind would wander. Sometimes I'd even fall asleep.

The people who prayed were nice enough, but the whole hand-holding thing drove me crazy. When the prayer would heat up, some of those spiritual warriors would start squeezing my hand harder and harder. If I was wearing a ring, it would dig into my other fingers and leave a painful mark. If you'd been there, you'd whine, too. (Except you, Todd.) One time I even asked a guy not to squeeze my hand so hard. He reminded me that Jesus suffered for me and that I shouldn't complain. I wanted to give him something to complain about.

Others had sweaty hands. That's just plain gross. Something seems very weird about holding a slimy hand while seeking God's heart. But nothing is as gross as the dead-fish hand. Every now and then someone would hold my hand so limply that it didn't deserve to be called a "grip"…completely lifeless. Even now the memory makes me shudder. I gotta tell you, these things aren't just amusing history for me. They *still* bother me.

Man, Craig, you're really shallow. Where's your spiritual passion?

I feel the same way. The truth is, I've never liked prayer meetings. Most of them are too long, too boring, and they involve more "sharing" than talking to God. I hate these meetings…and I have always been consumed with guilt because of it.

PATHETIC IN PRIVATE

I wish I could say that although I hate prayer meetings, I love private prayer, but I can't. My half-hearted, inconsistent, personal prayer life has always been a burden. In my years as a pastor, I've met many who can identify with my guilt-soaked, lackluster prayer life.

Why don't people like to pray? Well, for starters, many people don't know *how* to pray. Prayer seems intimidating, foreign, confusing. You don't want to say the wrong thing, or ask God for something that's off-limits. If you're like me, you feel your words are inadequate, not eloquent enough for the Creator of the universe. Many are just afraid of getting it wrong, so they don't pray at all.

Another reason people don't pray is they're not sure God will answer. Why bother? It seems like a waste of time. As a kid, I remember praying every night for my Grandpa Agee to be healed from cancer. I really believed that if I prayed hard enough, God had to answer my prayers and heal Agee. Grandpa Agee died. And I stopped praying for a long time.

Of course, one of the all-time most popular reasons for not praying is boredom. I pray "attention deficit disorder" prayers. The other night I was praying seriously and passionately. Suddenly I realized I needed to take out the garbage. *Speaking of garbage…I left the cheese wrapper on the drain board last night. Oh, yeah. We need more cheese…but my car is low on gas… and needs an oil change…when in the world will I get all this done?* Within seconds, I had forgotten I was even praying. Besides, with all those other things to do, who has time to pray? It scares me how quickly my mind wanders when I'm supposed to be fully focused on God.

And another reason people don't pray? They don't really think God cares. A teenage girl from church asked me once, "Why should I pray? God surely doesn't have time for my issues." I've felt that way before. God has to take care of countries filled with AIDS, starvation, wars, epidemics, and extreme poverty. Why would He care about my headache or my big assignment at work?

I hope you have a great prayer life. I know a lot of people who do, but I know many more who are like me: people with good intentions, but lacking follow-through. They genuinely love God but struggle at maintaining a growing and intimate relationship with Him.

For years I battled feelings of guilt. How can a Christ follower—especially a pastor—not be passionate about prayer? I deeply desired a more intimate relationship with God but didn't know how to develop it. Agonizing over my inadequacy, I wondered, *What's wrong with me?*

I think God eventually changed my heart simply because I clung to my desire for Him, even though I wasn't sure how to follow through on that desire. I pursued Him in my own halting, awkward, not-so-prayerful way. At some points through the long process, I felt like throwing in the towel, but in His strength, I continued. And He drew me closer and closer.

Day by day, over a period of years, I learned to relate personally with God…but not in a churchy, traditional, prayer-meeting type of relationship. I couldn't have tolerated that, and I don't think God would have, either. Not that God doesn't like those traditional relationships; He just knows that isn't what *I* like, and He wants me to enjoy my time with Him.

Your path toward an effective, fulfilling prayer life might be different from mine. But if you've struggled with consistency in prayer and devotion to God, maybe some of the things God has taught me will be helpful to you.

ENLARGE THE LIMITS

My most important breakthrough in learning to pray was to redefine prayer. In my mind, prayer was kneeling, hands clasped, in a church, or before a meal, or at bedtime. To me, prayer was always formal and stuffy. I had put prayer in a box. God deconstructed my box, and only then did prayer make complete sense to me.

The simplest definition of prayer is *communicating with God*.

That's it. Did you miss it? Let me say it again. Prayer is simply communicating with God. That one uncomplicated thought began to revolutionize my whole prayer life.

What is communication? It's transferring a thought, feeling, emotion, or idea to another person. So prayer is giving God my thoughts, feelings, emotions, and ideas, by whatever means works. It doesn't have to be formal. It doesn't have to be long and dry. It's simply communicating.

And communication doesn't even need words. If you were driving a car toward me and I held up my hand, palm open toward you, you'd know that I was asking you to *stop*. (And if you didn't, I'd be in trouble.) Then if I moved my hand a slightly different way, you'd know I was motioning you to *go*. If I pointed to the left or right, you would know which direction to turn. (Some drivers communicate quite powerfully with just one finger, but that's a subject we won't address in this book.)

My point is that we communicate every day without words. If prayer is communicating, then, sure, words work fine, but so do a hundred other methods. If you've been stuck in a prayer rut, break out of it. If you've been living on little or no prayer, that can change. Start by thinking about prayer differently: more simply, more intimately. Prayer is deep communication between two people—you and the One who made you and loves you.

DEMOLISH DISHONESTY

Let me introduce you to a guy who *really* prayed. He's the Old Testament prophet Jeremiah. If you look at his prayers, you'll likely agree that one word summarizes his communication: *honesty*.

Jeremiah never held back when talking with God. He got right to the point and said exactly what was on his mind. In Jeremiah 20:7, the prophet agonized in prayer, crying, "O LORD, you deceived me, and I was deceived; you overpowered me and prevailed. I am ridiculed all day long; everyone mocks me."

That's not the perfect specimen of a politically correct prayer, but Jeremiah didn't give a rip. This guy never played games with God. Neither should we.

Now, God didn't *really* deceive Jeremiah. But Jeremiah wasn't afraid to tell God about his subjective experience—what it felt like to him—without pulling punches.

Do you pray like that? For years I didn't dare. I used the Eddie Haskell approach to prayer. Remember Beaver's brother Wally's brownnosing friend on the TV show *Leave It to Beaver*? Every time Eddie would visit Beaver's house, he'd kiss up to the Beav's parents: "Hello, Mrs. Cleaver. You sure look lovely today." Eddie's words were right, but they probably weren't that genuine.

I prayed with the same formal, flattering dishonesty. (I occasionally still do.) I'd pray what I thought God wanted to hear, hoping to manipulate Him to my own ends. I prayed a flattering, polite, sterile type of prayer. I'm sure God wanted to say, "Will the real Craig Groeschel please stand up?"

Jesus wanted people to be real, not showy. He taught, "When you pray, do not be like the hypocrites, for they love to pray...*to be seen by men*" (Matthew 6:5, emphasis mine).

During his tenure as president, Lyndon Baines Johnson once asked Bill Moyers, a former Baptist minister who was on Johnson's staff, to pray before a meal. Mr. Moyers was honored to pray, but when he did, President Johnson couldn't hear him. The president asked Moyers to speak up so everyone could hear. Moyers replied, "I'm sorry. I wasn't talking to you, but to God."

One day it dawned on me why praying out loud made me nervous. I was praying to be seen and heard by people, not by God. Honestly, it was nothing short of hypocrisy. I cared more about what people thought than what God thought.

Pray honestly. What's on your mind right now? Are you hurting? Tell God about it, and allow His presence to start the healing. Are you afraid? Unload on Him, and you'll feel a lot lighter. Are you battling with doubts? Dump them on God, and you'll be surprised at the peace. Do you feel like God isn't being fair? Tell Him. Don't hold back. He can handle it. God wants you to be truthful with Him. Let it rip. Give Him your whole heart.

TOPICAL TOTALITY

"Does God care about my sick goldfish?" my six-year-old daughter asked.

Her question made me pause. *I don't really care about the goldfish. Why would God?* Then I noticed a tear begin its long, slow trek down my little girl's cheek. Because I cared for her, suddenly I cared for the stupid goldfish.

God is like that. Because He cares for you, He cares about what you care about. Paul seemed to know that God was into the details of our lives. He reminded the believers of Philippi, "Do not be anxious about anything, but in *everything*, by prayer and petition, with thanksgiving, present your requests to God" (Philippians 4:6, emphasis mine). Paul didn't say to pray only about the big, hairy, important-sounding things—but about everything.

I learned this lesson after returning from my honeymoon to a house with a broken air conditioner. It was the first week of July, and the temperatures were already over a hundred. Our first night together in our house, and it felt like an oven. My young bride, Amy, asked me to repair the decrepit machine.

How could I break the news to her? I couldn't repair squat. Not air conditioners. Not toasters. I couldn't even change our car's tire or oil. After explaining that air conditioners fall slightly beyond my area of expertise, she asked, "Well, have you prayed to God to fix it?"

Cornered!

Not only was I repair-challenged, now my new wife expected me to have the faith to ask God to fix the silly, inconsequential machine.

"No," I answered. "I guess I should pray." I tried to pretend I wasn't insulted by her outlandish request. I walked around to the AC unit in our backyard, feeling like a complete idiot. I glanced left, then right, to make sure no neighbors were looking. I stepped forward. *How do you pray for an air conditioner?* I remembered some Bible verse about laying hands on the sick. *Why not?* Placing my hands on the metal casing, I asked God to heal it.

Suddenly the air conditioner returned to life, cool air

streaming into the overheated house. (True story. Honest!) I ran inside, shouting and jumping for joy. "It worked! It worked! God answered my prayer!" Amy was excited, too. But she also gave me a look that said, *Didn't you know God could do it?*

Paul says we should pray about *everything* because God cares about everything—even your broken air conditioner, your stubbed toe, or your burned dinner. So pray about whatever's on your mind. Take it to Him. He cares for you.

Go ahead. Give it a try. Are you feeling lonely? *Talk* to God. Ask Him to be with you. Then *expect* to sense His presence. Are you stuck in a bind and don't know what to do? *Ask* Him for advice, like you'd ask a friend. Then allow Him to guide you step-by-step. Do you know someone who needs help, but you can only look on helplessly? *Petition* God. Watch Him intervene in ways you can't understand.

Pray about whatever concerns you. Anything. When everything is fair game, your prayer life can take off like a rocket toward heaven:

God, give me the words to say to this person.

God, give me patience.

God, bless her. Meet her needs.

God, use me to encourage him.

God, show me if I should buy this.

God, help me to see him as You do.

God, help me show her Your love.

Start now. Just talk to God…about everything.

And if your air conditioner's broken, e-mail me. I'll pray for it!

KEEP ON BREATHING

I'm very grateful to a woman who lived thousands of years ago. Her name was Hannah, and her story is in the Bible. Hannah's example sheds light on a Bible verse that used to frustrate the snot out of me. I didn't understand it, and it always made me feel guilty.

First Thessalonians 5:17 says, "Pray continually." The New King James Version translates it, "Pray without ceasing." Can you feel my angst? The Bible says to pray all the time, and I'm a pastor who struggles to enjoy prayer.

Have you ever desired something more than anything else, and not gotten it? Then you can relate to Hannah's plight. The desire of her life was to be a mom. She had prayed and begged God for years, with no results. Still, Hannah "kept on praying to the LORD" (1 Samuel 1:12). When everyone else told her it was no use, she kept praying. She never gave up.

You can imagine her frustration, always bringing pastel-wrapped gifts to her friends' baby showers. Everyone was getting pregnant—everyone but her. With no hope in sight, Hannah kept on praying. How often did she cry herself to sleep...God's name on her lips? Hannah prayed continually, and so should we.

After this woman prayed for who knows how long, God finally honored her prayers and gave her a miracle—a son she named Samuel (in whose honor we named our first son).

She prayed continually. I never could.

My knee-jerk reaction to the Bible's "pray continually" used to be: *I don't like to pray. My mind wanders and drifts. How can I pray continually when I can't even pray for five minutes straight?*

Great question. God answered it the day my two-year-old, Sam, wanted to ride his big sister's scooter. Now, I knew better than to put a two-year-old on something that is dangerous for a ten-year-old, but "knowing better" has never stood in the way of my stupidity.

The scooter was way too big for Sam, but he did amazingly well. I pushed him slowly across the flat part of the driveway. Exceptional balancing skills, perfect posture, excellent grip: *That's my boy!* I beamed with pride. *A chip off the old block.* I watched a future star athlete blossoming before my eyes. Having mastered level ground, Sam next wanted to go down our driveway's steep slope. You have to understand, it's pretty doggone steep. Even my older girls looked upon this challenge with grave reservations. It was a slope that would intimidate the bravest of souls.

So of course, I lined him up for the ride. Within seconds, he was flying, screaming down the slope at breakneck speed. A moment later he went FLYING. Literally. And screaming. Literally. Witnessing the sight of his two-year-old body smashing into the ground was one of the most appalling experiences of my life. Worse yet was the *crack*. I heard it from where I watched in horror. His femur snapped cleanly in two. We spent that night in the hospital, waiting for the operation that was scheduled for the morning. For ten long hours I held my little boy in my arms.

And I prayed without ceasing.

My prayer was never, "Dear God, blah blah blah blah." It was more like, *Oh, God, how could I have let this happen? How could I hurt my son? God, PLEASE, ease his pain. Help him stop crying. God, how is he going to handle a full-body cast for six weeks? Will this hurt him emotionally? Physically? Will he know it was my fault? Why, God? Help. Please forgive me. I feel horrible.* For ten hours I prayed, cried, agonized, and prayed some more.

With every breath, I exhaled a prayer. Eventually, Sam calmed down enough to sleep. The surgery was successful, and my now five-year-old is dangerously healthy again. From that night, I've carried the lesson of continuous prayer back to normal, daily life. Just as I needed God for the moment when Sam was in pain, I also need Him for all the rest of the moments in my life.

And so do you.

It's like my most important relationships. Hardly a day goes by that I don't make contact with them: e-mails, phone calls, text messages. I communicate with my mom and dad, my sister, and my closest friends. And I can't remember ever going twenty-four hours without talking to my wife and kids. If I'm traveling, I'll often call home several times a day.

Why do I make these contacts? Because I like to share my life with people who are significant to me. I like to hear their voices. I enjoy them. And when we communicate, I feel at peace, settled, more secure. I find the same peace and security—and more—when I stay in regular contact with God.

For me, continual prayer has become an *attitude*—not just a set of behaviors—directed to God. It's as if God is my constant travel companion. At times I chuckle as if He's chuckling with me. In the middle of some activity, I just say one sentence to Him, or I might talk for an hour at a time. This didn't come naturally at first, and often, I still forget to enjoy His presence. The good news is that even when we forget to pray continually, He never forgets to remain continually with us. (He's right there with you now. Amazing, isn't it?)

Since prayer is simply communication, I have available a wide range of ways to pray in different circumstances. Sometimes words. Sometimes thoughts. Sometimes just an awareness of His presence. The whole time, at every moment, He's there, ready to listen.

INNOVATIONS IN INTERCESSION

Speaking of variety, that brings me to my last thought on prayer. Even though I've learned to pray honestly, to pray about anything, and to pray continually, I'm still easily bored while praying. That's why a regular-guy-turned-king helped expand my understanding of prayer. The Bible tells the story of an ordinary shepherd boy with a heart for God who eventually became king of Israel. David's prayers lead me to pray *creatively*. God said David was a man after His own heart. I don't know anyone with a more inventive prayer and worship life. David prayed through his instruments of worship (Psalm 108:1–3), he prayed with songs (Psalm 13:6), he even prayed prayers while shouting (Psalm 20:5). You can, too. Have you ever turned your prayers into a song? I have. It's fun and freeing at the same time. You may say, "But I can't sing." Neither can I. That's what makes it so enjoyable. My singing is not for people, but for God.

David also played an instrument. You could, too. You could try some other variation on the prayer theme. While you're mowing your grass, you might pray for your neighbors. While you're jogging, you might pray for the people who live in the houses along the street, even if you don't know who they are. Sitting in a dull meeting at work, you can pray for your boss and all your coworkers who drive you crazy. You can take any ordinary activity and turn it into a moment of prayer.

David shouted to the Lord. Now, don't try that walking down a busy street. (I also tend to avoid this approach in restaurants and public restrooms.) But give it a shot at home. Shout praise to Him. Shout for joy. Even shout your hurts.

Pray creatively. I have a friend named Lori who tells God jokes (clean ones, of course). She even acknowledges that God has certainly heard them before, but this helps her feel close to Him. You see, Lori came from a legalistic background, believing that God was out to get her. By telling jokes to her Creator, Lori is growing in love with God.

Look at another one of David's prayers. In Psalm 5:1–2 he says, "Give ear to my words, O LORD, *consider my sighing*. Listen to my cry for help, my King and my God, for to you I pray" (emphasis mine).

I love the line, "consider my sighing." Have you ever thought about sighing as a form of prayer? *God, I love you…* pause…long sigh…pause…another deep, heartfelt sigh. God is so big, He understands the emotions, questions, pain, confusion, and hopes all wrapped up in your sighs. Now, you can't call just any old sigh a prayer, but a sigh directed toward God could become prayerful.

That's one way my wife communicates when we're sitting close. She might sigh a sigh of satisfaction, or a sigh of fear. Either way, in my love and understanding of her, I might pull her closer or say something encouraging—all because she sighed.

Pray creatively. Sigh. Shout. Sing. Or try something else. You might try:

+ **Writing your prayers.** That's what I do on Mondays. After a hard weekend of preaching, I sit at my com-

puter and talk to God in writing. Some weeks I write
a thank-you letter to God. Other weeks it's more like a
complaint letter. Sometimes it's like an e-mail to a close
friend. If you've never tried writing your prayers, grab a
pen, paper, laptop, Palm Pilot, or BlackBerry and pray
away.

+ **Praying during routine tasks.** Praying while com-
muting to work can make a long drive pleasurable and
valuable. (Just don't close your eyes. Remember, Jesus
said, "*Watch* and pray.") Maybe you can pray while
you're grocery shopping, doing the laundry, or working out at the gym. Turn your common activities into
uncommon time with your Father.

+ **Praying in different places.** I've got a favorite prayer
chair. I also have a special place in my yard that's holy
to me. You may enjoy praying in your office, in your
shower, or in your bed before sleeping or after you
wake up. You can clean out a closet and make a private
altar. Get out of the box and turn an ordinary place
into an extraordinary place for God.

+ **Varying your body's position.** One time, pray sitting.
Another time, try standing or walking. At times you
may enjoy the reverence of kneeling. Sometimes you
may be so overwhelmed by the glory and presence of

a holy God that you fall facedown on the floor.

+ **Praying by listening.** Remember our definition of prayer? It's communicating with God. Any good communication is two-way. Sometimes you need to shut up and listen. God wants to speak to you.

I'll never forget an awesome moment I had with my oldest daughter, Catie. When she was seven, she burst into my home office, beaming with excitement. "Daddy! Daddy!" she shouted. "God will tell you He loves you, if you listen closely enough."

I didn't understand, but I respected her passion and enthusiasm, so I asked her to tell me again. Smiling from ear to ear, she repeated herself word-for-word: "God will tell you He loves you, if you listen closely enough." Then she got very quiet and looked toward the heavens.

Pause.

(Still pausing.)

Then, glowing, she said slowly and deliberately, "See, I told you He would! You just have to listen closely." I'll be honest. I didn't hear anything at that moment…but I'm convinced that my sweet seven-year-old did.

God will speak to you, too. If you listen closely enough.

FREE AT LAST!

If you feel insecure about your faltering prayer life, I've got great news for you: God's waiting. Right now. At this moment. He wants to reveal Himself to you, and He wants you to reveal your heart to Him.

Pray. Pray creatively, openly, honestly. Pray long. Pray short. Sigh. Sing. Dance. Cry. Shout. Pray in the morning. During the day and in the evening. Pray in the car, while working, while doing chores. Laugh with Him. Cry with Him. Experience His presence. Let your attitudes, thoughts, energy, focus, attention, desire, and love be directed toward the One who loves you. Like breathing air, allow moment-by-moment fellowship to become a way of life—starting this very moment.

Go ahead. Communicate.

FIVE

I Worry Almost All the Time

P astors are supposed to exercise unwavering faith. No matter how circumstances appear, pastors should rest confidently in the faithfulness of God's faithfulness. When everyone else struggles with worry, the fearless pastor is expected to step in with just the right pastoral words.

It never seems to work that way for me.

Because of this picture we have of the ideal pastor—a concept I've apparently swallowed hook, line, and sinker— guilt plagues me as I agonize over this confession. But it's not just pastors who feel this way. Christians are expected to have great faith in a great God—worrying isn't supposed to be part of our lives, and we feel ashamed when it is. I know it makes me feel like an absolute spiritual failure. It haunts me and rarely goes away completely. The harsh reality is that even as a Christian, even as a pastor, I worry almost all the time.

I worry about big things, small things, important things, and silly things. Since God gives spiritual gifts, maybe His enemy gives spiritual curses. Worry is one of my curses. I worry...and worry...and worry...hating every minute of it.

One time I was visiting my friend, Dietmar, in Southern California. On the way from the airport to his condo, we got stuck in traffic on a major freeway. It was one of those double-decker freeways, where the top deck is built with tons and tons and tons of concrete and iron. The unimaginable bulk of the upper deck's construction might be reassuring to someone on the top deck. We were on the bottom deck. Surrounded by halted traffic. Waiting. For a long time.

That's about when Dietmar started describing California earthquakes to this Oklahoma boy. And I started to worry. My mind raced. *What if an earthquake hit right now? We'd be crushed under the weight of all that concrete. We'd be goners for sure. Squashed. Dead. No forwarding address. Do not pass go. Do not collect two hundred dollars.*

Somehow Dietmar sensed my concern. (I don't know. Maybe it was my profuse sweating, my rapid, shallow breathing, and my fingers digging into the armrests.) So he did what any good friend would do—he started messing with my mind.

"You know, they've been predicting an earthquake any day now," he started.

My heart skipped a beat. *He's just trying to scare me. They can't predict earthquakes...can they?*

"What was *that*?" Dietmar started glancing around, as though planning a route to safety. "Do you feel the ground shaking?" To this day, I'm certain I did.

Of course, there was no earthquake. But Dietmar enjoyed that experience for some time afterward.

As everyone knows, in the world of friendship, turnabout is fair play. A few months later, Dietmar visited my family's home. Helpful insight: Dietmar is even more afraid of tornadoes than I am of earthquakes. (God is so good.) My friend was getting comfortably settled in when I told him a tornado was on its way (even though it was seventy degrees without a cloud in the sky). I have video of Dietmar in our basement, crouching beneath an old mattress, bracing himself for a twister. Revenge is sweet.

Worry is not.

WHAT? ME RELAX?

You may be like me. Maybe you worry about the economy, your job, the health of someone you love, your aging parents, money, your kids' safety, your marriage, or terrorism. At different times I've been known to worry about all of these. Even when all is well, I generally worry about what bad thing is going to happen next.

Now, sometimes I worry about things I can change—I can provide part or all of the solution to the problem that's troubling me. When that's the case, I'm responsible for doing something about it. I need to take action. With some of your worries, so do you. This is a very important topic, so we'll come back to it later. However, my main burden is how to stop worrying about things we *can't* change. If you worry like me, let's journey together, and with God's help, learn to stop.

Some might argue, *What's the big deal, anyway? Everyone worries. It's a part of life. Accept it.* But I refuse to accept worry. It *is* a big deal. Not only does it do no good, it actually does a lot of harm. It hurts our bodies. It hurts our relationships. And it hurts our faith. Worry is a problem. Worse, it's a sin.

Someone defined worry as "the sin of distrusting the promises and power of God." When I worry, I'm telling God by my actions and attitude that I don't trust Him. Even though I claim to believe He is all-powerful, ever-present, and all-knowing, when I worry, I'm saying I don't think He can handle what's bothering me. That must be a real insult to my heavenly Father's heart. I don't like to insult my Father.

In the past few years, with intentional and prayerful work, I've made significant progress growing in my trust in God—but not nearly enough. I'll walk you through my journey and share some things I've learned—and am *still* learning. If constant worry is holding you back, I pray you'll grow out of it faster than I have.

INHERITED DEPRESSION

My grandma was an amazing person. Before she died, she had a huge positive influence on my life. I'm thankful for a thousand things she taught me. She encouraged me. She inspired me. She helped me to think big. But she also taught me to worry.

Grandma grew up during the Great Depression—an experience that profoundly shaped her perspective on life. She endured extreme poverty and often didn't know where she would find her next meal. The survival instincts she developed stayed with her throughout her adult life.

When I was seven years old, Grandma told me about the horrors of the Depression. With contagious passion, she recounted stories about people who lost everything overnight. Some jumped from windows. Others lived under bridges. Many never recovered. With the purest motives, she told me I needed to save money. She told me to be prepared always... because one day the economy *would* fall apart again. It might happen that very year. Or the next. Or in ten years. But it *was* going to happen again, and because she loved me, she didn't want me or my loved ones to go hungry.

Those words planted a seed of worry in my young heart that began to sprout and blossom. I became the child prodigy of worry. I worried big...especially about money. If Grandma gave me ten dollars for my birthday, I never spent a penny of it. I hid every dollar I received or earned under the carpet in my bedroom. I knew someday the economy would come crashing down, and I'd need that cold, hard cash to help the family buy bread.

Grandma's lessons benefited me in many ways. I've never borrowed money for anything but a house. I've only bought affordable homes and paid them off quickly. Yet to this day, I fight my financial anxieties. Even though I'm debt-free, I still *worry*: What happens if it all falls apart?

My financial fears have needlessly hurt my family. My worry shows up in weird ways and at weird times. I refuse to buy soft drinks, opting instead for water (which *is* better for you—but I drink it mostly because it's free). If cheese on a hamburger is an extra eighty cents, I usually go without. (You never know when you might need an extra eighty cents.)

A few years ago, I took my oldest daughter out for her birthday. We went to her favorite tearoom. Catie read down the menu, skipping over her favorite meal and settling on the cheapest item available. When I asked her why she didn't order her favorite, she replied quietly, "I'm afraid we can't afford it."

I was crushed. We are in excellent financial shape. But the same fear I learned from my grandma, I had inadvertently passed down to my daughter. That was the moment when I decided to break free from worry about money. I refuse to pass along my weaknesses and sins to my children.

Unchecked worry will have nothing but detrimental effects in your life. If you worry about your spouse's fidelity, your very attitude is almost certain to cause marital conflict. If you worry about your kids' safety, it may hurt your own health. If you're consumed with worry about your future, you may miss out on living today. Most of all, if you continue to live gripped by worry, you'll miss the glory of knowing and trusting God's goodness.

HOW TO MAKE A BAD DAY WORSE

God wants us to trust Him because as our faith expands, worry shrinks. My faith is starting to grow. What progress I've made has only come as I've internalized His truth. When I apply His truth, rather than giving in to anxiety, I live in His peace, which surpasses my understanding. When I don't, I live paralyzed by worry and fear.

The first thing God's taught me is *to take my mind off the "what ifs" of worry*. For years I played the what-if game. Maybe you're acquainted with this pastime. The rules are simple:

- Rule #1: You're only allowed to think of worst-case scenarios.

- Rule #2: You're never allowed to win this game. You can only lose.

• Rule #3: The more you play, the greater your losses.

Here are a few excerpts from my own game played over the years: *What if something bad happens to one of my kids? What if our house catches on fire? What if I lose my job? What if I get cancer? Or worse yet…what if someone I love gets cancer?*

What's weird to me is that my what-ifs always seem to be negative. I rarely ask, *What if something great happens?*

I've had to make up my mind not to focus on the fearful what-ifs. That's what Jesus taught. In Luke 21, Jesus warned his disciples about future hardships. He foretold false prophets, earthquakes, famines, pestilence, and wars. He told his followers they would suffer and be persecuted. From my perspective, these are things worthy of worry…but not to Jesus. He told them to "make up your mind not to worry beforehand" (v. 14). I love the way He worded His statement. "Make up your mind." Decide ahead of time. Before anything happens, decide not to worry. Don't dwell on what could go wrong. Trust Him. Don't play the what-if game.

For years, whenever my wife was late coming home, I'd play the what-if game. *What if she was in a car accident? What if she's hurt badly? Or…gulp…what if she's been killed?* If you promise not to stop reading, I'll tell you how far down I'd let worry take my mind. Since my losses in the beginner and intermediate levels of the what-if game brought no solutions or satisfaction, I'd advance to the expert level. Panicking, sick to my stomach, I'd proceed on the assumption that she'd never again walk through the front door. *Will I be able to perform her funeral? No way. How could I? What's going to become of our six kids without their mom? And me? Who would marry a guy with six kids?* I hope your brand of worry isn't industrial-strength like mine. But I know a lot of people who worry at all different levels, and not one of them ever wins the game.

I heard about a young woman who was a chronic worrier. She worried about the weather. She worried about her family. She worried when there was nothing to worry about. This worrier had a wise father who finally said to her, "Come over this afternoon, and we'll sit together for an hour and just worry."

Without thinking, the daughter blurted out, "That's the stupidest thing I've ever heard! Sitting around for an hour worrying won't do any good."

Suddenly it dawned on her: She was wasting precious time and energy doing something that obviously didn't work.

Let's be honest. Worry never changes anything for good, so why should we waste our lives doing something so useless? Jesus even asked the question, "Who of you by worrying can add a single hour to his life?" (Matthew 6:27). In fact, almost every time I see worry mentioned in the Bible, it has two words in front of it: *Do not.*

What if I told you that by worrying, we're playing into the plan of our spiritual enemy? The evil one's tool of fear is meant to distract us from God's best. Fear and worry are a lot like a scarecrow. What harm can a scarecrow do? We scarecrow constructors know that the answer is "none," but the birds don't know that.

You're smarter than a bird. That's why the prophet Jeremiah says that some of the enemy's greatest threats are "like a scarecrow in a melon patch.... Do not fear them; they can do no harm" (Jeremiah 10:5). Then he refocuses our attention where it belongs: "No one is like you, O LORD; you are great, and your name is mighty in power" (v. 6).

If those black birds ever figured out our strategy, they'd realize that a scarecrow is actually a tip-off to the location of the best corn. So, isn't it possible that the very fears the enemy tries to plant in your mind are unwitting advertisements for God's good stuff? (Like a "Danger" sign on God's cookie jar.) Worry keeps you from God's best. So take your mind off the what-ifs that grow out of fear.

THINKING BETWEEN THE TREES

Not only am I learning to take my mind off of the negative possibilities of life, but I'm also learning to put my mind *onto* something—God's promises. We must replace our fearful, consuming thoughts with reminders of God's faithfulness.

Extreme skiing is a wild sport. The participants are talented, half-crazy athletes, known for flying down mountains at kamikaze speeds. With every outing, they risk becoming the new "agony of defeat" guy, crashing head over heels, limbs bending every which way like a sadistic child's Gumby doll.

Kim Reichhelm is one of the best and has miraculously escaped serious harm. Someone asked her once, "How do you keep from crashing?"

Her answer, "I look at the spaces between the trees." Brilliant. Instead of looking at what she didn't want to hit, she aimed her eyes where she wanted to go—away from danger, toward safety and success.

Similarly, instead of focusing on the worst-case scenarios— my natural programming—I'm learning to look at the spaces between the trees. That's where I see God's promises of security, blessing, protection, provision, guidance, wisdom, and love. Between the trees lies God's path, and on His path, there's no need for worry.

I've tried to imagine what my doubts must do to God's heart. When I'm focusing on the trees, that means I'm not focusing on Him, not trusting Him. How does that make Him feel? I got a small glimpse at a pizza arcade once.

When my first son, Sam, was three years old, I took him to a Chuck E. Cheese restaurant. Chuck E. Cheese is one of my kids' favorite places for me to spend way too much money. It's a pizza and game room combined with a mascot mouse named—you guessed it—Chuck E.

Chuck E. is pretty cute, if you ask me. He doesn't look threatening in the least. But for some reason I've never understood, Sam was terrified to death of Chuck E. I exercised all my skills of fatherly encouragement and reassurance trying to get Sam to go give the overgrown mouse a hug. It simply wasn't happening.

"He's really nice," I told Sam. "Go give him a hug."

Sam wouldn't budge. Finally I told him to wait where he was and watch Daddy go talk to Chuck E. Approaching the fur-and-whisker-clad guy, I said to him quietly, "My son's afraid of you. Do you mind if I push you gently and show him you won't attack me?" Chuck E. nodded the affirmative, willing to play along.

I made sure Sam was watching (from a distance) as I ever-so-slightly pushed Chuck E. I wasn't prepared when Chuck E. pushed me back. It was all in fun, so I lightly popped him on the head. He popped me on the head even harder with his paw. I popped him back, harder. He swung at me. Please understand that I was only playing, and I'm fairly certain the humanoid rodent was, too. But before I knew it, I had Chuck E. in a headlock. It was all very innocent, but some other small kid recognized me and yelled, "Pastor Craig is beating up Chuck E.!"

Sam never would approach the mouse. Thanks to my efforts, maybe he never will. The point of this silly story is that Sam wouldn't take me at my word. (Granted, he was only three.) But I'm his dad. I promised him he'd be safe, and he didn't believe me.

I wonder how God feels when we don't take Him at his word. When we distrust His power and promises. When we worry instead of believing Him. George Mueller said it best: "The beginning of anxiety is the end of faith, and the beginning of true faith is the end of anxiety." Think about it. Worry brings turmoil. Faith brings peace. Worry takes you from God. Faith draws you to God. Worry changes nothing. Faith moves God's heart and can change everything for the better.

I'm training my mind to focus on God's promises. The prophet Isaiah makes a powerful promise to us when he says to God, "You will keep in perfect peace him whose mind is steadfast, because he trusts in you" (Isaiah 26:3).

Don't play the what-if game. Focus on God's promises.

TUG-OF-WAR WITH GOD

Here's another thing I'm learning: to give my cares to God and not take them back. This one's easier said than done. You wouldn't believe how often I pray something like, *God, I know You can do all things, so I give this problem to You. I trust You to handle it.* Then five minutes later, I'm worrying again or trying to manipulate the situation.

Between the ages of fifteen and seventeen, I was a passenger in three separate car accidents. The third time, the driver of the car I was in ran a stop sign at a highway intersection. A

Blazer struck my side of the car at fifty-five miles per hour. Ever since then, I've been frightened to ride as a passenger, and I rarely do. As a driver, I've never had a traffic ticket or a wreck. My wife calls me "Grandpa driver." I call it wise discretion.

I always want to be in control of the car. When someone else is driving, I tend to offer obnoxious advice, because my survival instinct cries out for some kind of control. Sometimes I have to surrender control and trust the outcome to someone else, but this doesn't come naturally to me.

With God, the "control" I have to surrender over and over is only an illusion. I never really have control of my life and circumstances, even when I pretend to.

Have you acknowledged that truth? You're not in control. You never have been.

If that's true—and it is—then why do we try to exercise power that has never been ours? (That was a rhetorical question, but the answer has a lot to do with human pride.)

When I finally get around to genuinely trusting the only One who's in control, I discover amazing comfort. God never panics. I love that. Never in history has God said, "Wow, I didn't see that coming. What in the galaxy am I going to do now?" God knows more about what you're worried about than you do. And He...is...in...control.

Can anyone *completely* trust God and be free from *all worry*? I'm not sure if that's humanly possible. That said, my wife is the closest person I know to being truly worry free. She's filled with a genuine faith that I envy—but she wasn't born that way.

After giving birth to our second child, Amy faced some unusual health challenges. Sometimes the whole right side of her body would go numb. Her doctors were concerned about her future health and safety, and they gave her every kind of test you can imagine. They couldn't find the cause, but they took every precaution. In her mind, she became convinced she was dying. Fear took complete control. She couldn't sleep for days at a time, and she'd cry, terrified.

I didn't know what to do. Only one word described my feelings: *helpless*. My prayers didn't seem to work. I didn't know what to say. Like my wife, I was off-the-charts worried. Hundreds of people were praying for her. Then, one day, as suddenly as the numbness had begun, it left. We never knew why it came or why it went...but we know the One who brought the cure.

During that time of suffering and fear, Amy spent many deep, intimate hours and days with her heavenly Father. At last, she came to a point of surrender and trust that's hard to describe. That's when she learned almost complete freedom from worry. I feel chills every time she describes her journey of faith.

Amy doesn't worry today because God allowed her to face her greatest fear—the fear of dying, of leaving her babies and her husband. She explains through tears that her only prayer during her illness was to live. For months she begged God to let her live. Finally she chose a different prayer. She surrendered everything to God and told Him that if He wanted to take her, she would rejoice to meet Him face-to-face. In that moment, she burst free from the grip of worry.

When I tell you that Amy doesn't worry, I mean it. She doesn't worry. It amazes me. On September 11, 2001, guess where I was while hijackers crashed four airplanes full of passengers? On an airplane. And Amy? Not for a minute did she worry about me. When I asked her why, she told me simply and confidently, "I trust God. He's not through with you yet, so why should I worry? And even if He took you, He's still good. You're in His hands. I have nothing to worry about." She meant it. Amy learned to give her cares to God and not take them back. I long to become more like that.

If you do, too, here's a great exercise for you. Find a box (or any other container) and write the words "Trusting God" on it. You might even get wild and call it your "Trusting God" box. Whenever you're worried about something you can't change, write your worry on a piece of paper and put it in the box. Once it's inside the box, it becomes God's property, His responsibility, not yours (it never was). From the moment you give your problem to Him, you're not allowed to worry about it. If you want to worry, then you have to go to the box and physically take the concern away from God. And when you do, you'll visually and physically act out what's really happening inside—you're choosing to stop trusting God.

Why not go find yourself a "Trusting God" container right now? While you're at it, scribble down two or three of your heaviest burdens and drop them in. It'll only take a couple of minutes. Then come back, and we'll pick up where we left off.

I BELIEVE THIS MIGHT BE YOURS?

As I said earlier, throughout most of this chapter, I've chosen to focus on worries we can't do anything about. What about the other worries—the ones where the solution lies at least partially in our hands? Don't stop trusting God for these, and don't stop praying about them. But God has entrusted responsibility to us, and He wants us to take it…starting now.

Worried about money? Deal with your debt. Write a budget. Save. Do something. Are you worried about someone finding out about your secret affair? That's a legitimate worry. You can do something about it. It's time to come clean. Are you worried about your weight? Step away from the ice cream sundae, and no one will get hurt.

If you *can* do something about your worries, by all means, *do*, and do it in God's wisdom and power. If something in this category comes to mind, take action as soon as you finish this chapter (if not sooner). However, if your worry is completely out of your control…

Stop playing the what-if game.

Learn and think about God's promises.

Give your concerns to God—then don't take them back.

If anyone had reason to worry, it was the apostle Paul. Yet from a Roman prison, awaiting his possible execution, he penned these words: "Do not be anxious about anything, but in everything, by prayer and petition, with thanksgiving, present your requests to God. And the peace of God, which transcends all understanding, will guard your hearts and your minds in Christ Jesus" (Philippians 4:6–7).

In other words, *Pray about everything. Worry about nothing.* Whatever's on your mind is also on God's heart. Take it to Him. Then leave it with Him. He cares. He's your Father—a Father like no other on earth.

Pray about your upcoming test. Pray for your presentation at work. Pray about what to say on your first date. Pray about your granddaughter's sick hamster. Or pray about finding your lost keys. (I pray that at least twice a week.) Pray about everything, and worry about nothing.

Are you living with worry? Does it dominate your life? Consume your waking hours? Steal your sleep? I've lived most of my life like that—but God is setting me free.

"Cast all your anxiety on him because he cares for you" (1 Peter 5:7).

One day I went to the gym with my workout partner, John. We were doing chest exercises. On our final rounds, we did a burnout session. That's when you completely exhaust the muscles by doing as many repetitions as humanly possible. John was spotting me on the bench press as I dropped a rather light weight on and off my chest. For a minute or so the weight seemed…well, weightless. Then my oxygen-deprived muscles started to labor, and the weight felt heavier and heavier.

John urged me on. "IT'S ALL YOU! IT'S ALL YOU!" He started supporting the weight for me.

"IT'S ALL YOU! IT'S ALL YOU!" he shouted, taking more of the weight as I weakened.

Finally, I gave up completely and let go of the bar, but John didn't notice. He kept lifting the weight off my chest and lowering it again, shouting the whole time, "IT'S ALL YOU! IT'S ALL YOU!"

Then he realized what he was doing. We both cracked up laughing. John was carrying the whole burden of the bar and weight, but only after I let go. What weight in your life feels like it's "all you"? Take a break. You can rest once you realize that it's all God.

Always has been.

SIX

Sometimes I Doubt God

My first memorable spiritual hiccup was a time I doubted the existence of God. It happened, oddly enough, in church. I was probably seven or eight years old. The minister was preaching…and I was bored.

Without warning, the question dropped into my mind: *Is God real? Or is He just something we made up?* Fear and guilt overwhelmed me immediately. I tried to ignore the question and listen to the rest of the boring sermon.

But my doubts didn't go away.

Is God real? If He is, is He good? With all the bad things that happen in the world, it's sometimes hard to believe He's involved, or even there at all. My bout with doubt continued through childhood into my teens. It crept up occasionally while I was in seminary. It's bothered me even as a minister.

Is it so unreasonable to expect God to do a few small things to help everyone believe in Him? A modern-day burning bush (that's never consumed) would be cool. Parting the ocean or allowing a whale to swallow a runaway prophet, only to puke him out on the shore, would be impressive (caught on amateur video, of course). Move a mountain. Raise a dead guy to life. Anything dramatic would do the trick. Even though God can and has acted with such power—and much more—He doesn't seem to do as much of that today.

That's always confused me, so as a kid I gave God ample opportunities to prove Himself. Each time, I made Him a deal, offering Him a payoff I didn't think He could refuse. *God, if You just prove Yourself, I'll serve You for the rest of my life.* Or, *I'll go to Africa as a missionary.* Or, *I'll give more money to poor people.*

The first opportunity I gave God to prove Himself involved a picture of Jesus—the classic picture of the Savior with long blond hair and blue eyes (exactly the opposite traits from those of any Jewish person I know). The picture was hanging above my twin bed.

One night before falling asleep, I tilted the picture askew, and I prayed one small request: *God, just make the picture straight while I'm sleeping.* If it was straight in the morning, I'd know God was real, and then, of course, He could have me for the rest of my life. I've never been so eager to fall asleep.

In the morning, the picture was still crooked.

Some years later, during my sophomore year of high

school, I made God yet another deal, this time at youth camp. My buddies had smuggled some beer and a *Sports Illustrated* swimsuit magazine on the trip. (Believe it or not, I had more opportunities per square inch to sin on church trips than I did at home.) Even though I didn't like beer, I drank some just to fit in…and of course, I looked at the magazine. The next day in chapel, all my sinful friends and I were feeling guilty for drinking beer and looking at girls in bikinis while at church camp.

One of the youth counselors challenged us to spend two hours alone with God. I'd never done anything like that before, but in this guilt-filled moment, I actually thought it was a good idea. Bible in hand, I walked alone into the woods, hoping to meet with God. Still filled with doubts about the reality of God, I wrestled back and forth in my mind: *Why do I feel bad about doing these things? It must be because there is a God. But then again, I could just be imagining the whole thing. Maybe I just want to believe in God because my parents do.* It was time to give God another chance to prove Himself. The Jesus-picture thing flopped, but maybe a new proposal would be more attractive to God. This time, in the middle of a heavily wooded area, I took two small sticks and put them in front of me in the form of a cross. Just to sweeten the pot, I upped my side of the bargain. With not much more than a mustard seed's worth of faith, I told God, *If You just move one of these sticks, not only will I give You my life, but I'll become a minister.* How could God refuse such a generous offer?

I started praying and believing. And praying. And believing. Waiting patiently. Two hours later, both sticks lay motionless on the ground, still forming the shape of a cross. Crushed with disappointment, I went back to my cabin, drank some more beer, and looked at pictures of girls in bikinis.

A SEEDLING'S STRUGGLE
FOR SURVIVAL

Early in college I never went to church. Honestly, I didn't seem to be missing much. God wasn't even on my radar. If grades were based on partying and chasing girls, I would have been valedictorian.

At one point, after my fraternity got in a lot of trouble, I started attending a Bible study. Again God began to draw me to Himself. In the middle of the grossest and most blatant sins of my life, I started to pray. The prayers were pretty rough—mostly about God keeping me safe when I drove drunk and not letting my girlfriends get pregnant.

Then one day, it happened. I can't fully explain it, and I feel inadequate trying. But somehow, in some way, God's presence became as real to me as the laptop I'm typing on. He didn't straighten a picture of Jesus or move any twigs. He was simply *with* me. Not in some creepy, scary-movie sort of way, but in the most loving, accepting, and life-changing way I can imagine. I wasn't in church. No other person was there. It was just me lying facedown on a vacant softball field. Praying. Seeking. And hoping.

Without Me you have nothing. With Me you have everything.

Those were the words I heard. Not audibly. They were much too loud to be audible. They were on the inside, and they were very real. At that moment, I prayed my first unconditional, no-strings-attached prayer of absolute surrender. *Okay, God, I believe. Take my whole life.*

He did. Overnight, God changed me.

My school records said I majored in business marketing, but at heart I became a minister—not by choice, but *by calling*. Ministering to others was not just one of the things I did; it began to define *my identity*. With every bone in my body, I believed in God. My faith was unshakable, my devotion wholehearted. No more doubts. Never again.

At least for a while.

For several years my faith remained strong. I graduated from college, got married, and started full-time ministry at the age of twenty-three. One year later, while serving a local church, I enrolled in cemetery. Whoops! I meant to say *seminary*. Well, actually, I meant to say both. The sad truth is that many people bury their faith under a monument called "Religious Education." That's what almost happened to me.

I thought seminary would build my faith. Instead, I was shocked to find that it reawakened my old doubts, and the person who raised the most questions was my New Testament professor. On the first day of class, Dr. Miles (not his real name) threw the Bible at the wall and said, "That's what I think of this book." Then he promised to shred our naïve faith and undo all of our simple-minded beliefs. He did a pretty good job. Dr. Miles didn't believe Jesus said most of what is recorded in the Gospels. He thought Paul wrote only a select few epistles, and he thought John was either stoned or suffering from bad gas when he wrote the book of Revelation. By the time I turned in my final exam, my faith was hanging by a thread.

Please understand that not all seminaries are like this one. I've since attended a different school and had a dramatically different experience. But that first one almost destroyed my faith. Thankfully, I had a different professor the next semester who believed the Bible literally. Not only did he believe, but he was brilliant. He taught me that I could be a thinking person and still believe that God's Word can stand the test of time and the criticism of man, that science confirms Scripture, and that you don't have to duck hard questions. I learned that I didn't have to defensively protect God or His Word, but that I could trust both. I believed. Again. Unshakable, steadfast, forever.

Until something else would rattle my faith.

BREEDS OF BELIEF

On again, off again. Some days spiritually confident and strong, other days inwardly unsure and insecure. I've come a long way since then, and my rollercoaster faith has leveled out considerably. I'm still not free from all doubts, but I've climbed a long and difficult path. From here the view is a lot clearer, and my confidence in God is more solid and lasting.

As I look back, I realize that part of the difference has to do with the distinction between believing *in* something and *believing* it. For example, I have a friend who believes in airplanes, but he's afraid to fly. He says planes are a good thing, but he doesn't believe they will carry him safely to his destination.

Similarly, there's a big difference between believing *in* God and *believing* God. James reflected this truth when he wrote, "You believe that there is one God. Good! Even the demons believe that—and shudder" (James 2:19). Demons know God is real, but they obviously don't serve Him. For years I tried to believe *in* God without fully *believing* Him.

There are at least three types of faith on the spectrum between "believing in" and "believing," and I've experienced them all. The first kind of faith is held by the person I call the *casual* believer. Such a person believes in God, but hasn't fully surrendered to Him. He may be a church attender, and possibly a very moral person. Even though this person believes in God, he lives his life as if God doesn't really exist—a confessing theist, but a practicing atheist.

Many people I know are casual believers. They'll pray a polite prayer at Thanksgiving meals, attend church on Christmas and Easter, and tell you they're "thinking about you" during difficult times. But these same people don't let God affect their spending habits or the movies they watch. He doesn't slow their selfish sexual appetites, keep them from cursing on the golf course, or stop them from fudging on an expense report, gossiping, stretching the truth, or telling a white lie to get ahead. They believe in God, but they still do pretty much whatever they want.

Maybe you know a casual believer. Or maybe this description fits you.

The second type of faith is that of the *convenient* believer. This is one who waves the Christian flag whenever it involves a potential benefit. The convenient believer is quick to talk God-talk if it might help seal a business deal, or score a date, or land a promotion. This person uses God to leverage a situation for personal benefit.

In college I met a convenient believer at a fraternity party. I was a new Christ follower and ready to be a good witness. Suddenly a very drunk freshman girl came up and threw herself at me. She was, shall we say, "very friendly." When I told her, "I'm not going there; I'm a Christian," she immediately tried to sober up. She told me she was a Christian, too. In fact, she was the next Amy Grant. Then she started singing an alcohol-slurred rendition of a Christian song. She hadn't stopped her sexual advances; she'd only switched to a sanitized approach. Her faith was a convenient faith.

The third type of faith belongs to the *committed* believer.

And this is what Jesus calls us toward. The road to committed faith is paved with personal abandonment and self-denial. Life ceases to be about us, and it begins to be all about God. The committed believer doesn't waver because of the crowd. He isn't moved by others' opinions. He's a Christ follower all the time. Complete obedience and faithfulness are his goals. A 99 percent commitment to Christ is not enough.

This reminds me of the story of a famous tightrope walker named Jean François Gravelet, who was known professionally as the Great Blondin. Blondin was famous for balancing on thin wires and walking across just about any chasm. No height or stunt was too great. Once, in front of a huge crowd, he tightrope walked across Niagara Falls. One reporter applauded his success and said enthusiastically, "I bet you could even do that pushing a wheelbarrow." Sure enough, Blondin did. The reporter was blown away and exclaimed: "I bet you could even walk across with a person in the wheelbarrow." Blondin replied, "If you're so sure, hop in the wheelbarrow. You can be that person." The reporter declined.

God wants us to hop in His wheelbarrow with full-blown, sold-out faith.

So what kind of faith is yours? Casual belief—you're a good person who believes in God, but doesn't let your faith dominate your life? Convenient belief—living right when someone's watching, or when it might benefit you, but doing your own thing when you want?

Or are you committed—wholly devoted to the One who's wholly devoted to you?

AN HONEST HERO

You may think, *I want to be committed, but I still struggle with so many doubts.* What do you do when you don't fully believe? I can't tell you how often I face this question.

I've found great comfort and a stronger faith in the story of a fellow doubter. His name was Thomas (perhaps you know him as Doubting Thomas). Like me, he was a guy who didn't fully believe. You've probably heard his story, and you may have seen some of yourself in him—and felt guilty because of it. But you might be surprised to find that Thomas's journey from doubt to faith can strengthen your own belief. And if you look with fresh eyes, you may even find that for centuries, Thomas has gotten a bad rap for his doubts.

Thomas was most likely a fisherman, in charge of the family business. Upon meeting Thomas, the Messiah offered him the chance of a lifetime. Instead of fishing for fish, he could change the world by fishing for men. So Thomas, like all of the disciples, left everything to follow Jesus (see Matthew 19:27). He walked away from family, from a profitable business, from whatever home he had built—everything—all because he *believed* in the One who called him.

Thomas didn't doubt...at least not at first.

After three years teaching His disciples, the Son of God gave His life on a cross. And Thomas's world went dark. Three days later, the word on the street was *Egerthe!* In Greek, that means, "He is risen!" According to some women who claimed to have seen Him, Jesus was alive! I imagine that everything in Thomas wanted to believe that Jesus had returned from the grave and defeated sin. But like so many others, Thomas doubted.

I might be in the minority, but I'd argue that Thomas's doubts were one of his greatest assets. Yes, you read that right. Sincere doubts, handled properly, can become a gift. This is as true for you as it was for Thomas. If you have occasional—or even regular—bouts with doubts, your sincere struggle to believe may leave your faith stronger than if you'd never questioned it.

What did Thomas do in his struggle to reach committed belief? Well, one thing he did was *acknowledge his doubts.* In John 20:25, Thomas said to the other disciples, "Unless I see the nail marks in his hands and put my finger where the nails were, and put my hand into his side, I will not believe it."

I find his honesty incredibly refreshing. In most of the churches I've been around, sincere doubting is frowned upon. Thomas didn't care what anyone thought. He put it all on the line and said, "God has to prove it to me." Instead of shaming him for his doubts, I want to congratulate Thomas for understanding the significance of the event. Thomas knew that if Jesus had risen, everything would forever be different. He refused to take someone else's word for it. Thomas had to experience it for himself.

For years, I took someone else's word about the reality of God. Instead of personally investigating, I believed because my parents believed. I accepted what my Sunday school teachers told me. I followed my pastors' belief. That was fine in my childhood, but as I neared adulthood, it wasn't enough. My belief had to be *my* belief. I had to own it. It had to come out of my seeking, my experience.

Thomas was unwilling to settle for second-hand when first-hand experience was a possibility. I can almost feel his passion and hear his thoughts: *If Jesus is alive, then everything He said was true! Life won't be about what we see, but about what we can't see. The kingdom of God is here. I'm called to be a light in the world. If Jesus has risen, the gospel demands my entire life. I MUST know for myself!*

Some people say, "The Bible says it, I believe it, and that settles it." I'm sincerely happy for their faith. Mine has never been that simple. Maybe you can relate. Do you have doubts? Questions? Hesitations? I challenge you to pursue a course you'll rarely hear a pastor endorse—ask the hard questions:

Do I believe because my parents believed?

Is my "faith" just a way of coping with my weakness?

Is Christianity just a myth?

What about other world religions? Is Jesus the only way to God?

SOMETIMES I DOUBT GOD

Did He really rise from the dead?

Did someone just make this whole thing up?

Thomas wasn't afraid to ask the hard questions. And we shouldn't be, either.

But Thomas did more. Next he *pursued the answers*. We pick up his story in John 20:26–27: "A week later [Jesus'] disciples were in the house again, and Thomas was with them. Though the doors were locked, Jesus came and stood among them and said, 'Peace be with you!' Then he said to Thomas, 'Put your finger here; see my hands. Reach out your hand and put it into my side. Stop doubting and believe.'"

Thomas didn't stop at just asking questions; he didn't become stuck, circling in a holding pattern of skepticism. He continued exploring, and his honest pursuit of truth took him straight to the risen Savior. Faith grows when we seek answers to the right questions. We find answers through passionately pursuing truth. Many people just ask the questions...then go no further.

Take my friend Mike. Mike believes in God, but doesn't trust Him. While I desperately wish he'd cross the boundary between the two, I can empathize with his struggles. When Mike was twelve, he found his mom dead in the bathtub. She had drowned during an epileptic seizure. At that moment, Mike says, he lost his faith in God. *How could a good God allow that to happen? Why does God let bad things happen to good people? Why doesn't God seem fair?*

If you haven't had a major, life-shaking event yet, buckle your seatbelt. When yours happens, you'll see how easy it is to voice your pain through questions. Questions by themselves can become barriers to faith. But questions that lead to answers are pathways to God Himself.

DOUBT: FAITH'S FOUNDATION

My thirty-four-year-old brother-in-law David died in 2004. To me, that didn't seem fair. The experience caused my family profound grief. Still, it didn't shake my faith. Instead, my faith grew stronger. Why? Because years ago I asked a hard question: *Why doesn't God seem fair?*

As a young pastor I recognized way too many injustices: a young child killed in a car accident while the drunk driver walked away unharmed; a godly couple who couldn't have children while others aborted multiple lives; rich people living in luxury while thousands die daily of starvation.

Why, God? It doesn't seem fair.

After asking the hard question, I sought the answer. And God revealed Himself to me through Scripture. Here's the answer He gave me: *I'm not fair. You should be thankful I'm not.* You read that right: God is not fair, and that is good news to us.

Now, before you run down the street yelling, "Craig Groeschel is smoking pot!" let's think about this together. God is *just*—no doubt about it—but He's not *fair*. And there is a difference. If God were fair, I'd get what my sins deserve. I praise Him that He's not fair. Because He's just, when someone sins, someone must die. But in His mercy, Jesus paid the price for my sin by shedding His own innocent blood, giving up the life He fully deserved to keep. God is just, but He's not fair. If He were fair, I'd have to suffer…forever. Psalm 103:10, 12 describes God's unfairness: "He does not treat us as our sins deserve or repay us according to our iniquities.… As far as the east is from the west, so far has he removed our transgressions from us."

When my brother-in-law died, it didn't seem fair, but through his untimely death, my wife's uncle came to know Christ. So did dozens of others. Now they'll experience the same heavenly reality that David is enjoying at this moment.

Many people don't see all the beautiful implications of God's unfairness. What they do see looks ugly to them and causes their faith to falter. I've spent a lot of time trudging through that swamp of confusion, asking lots of questions. Over time, God has shown me His answers and has bolstered my faith. I hope I never again have to wrestle with doubts about God's fairness. But still, other doubts hang in the wings of my mind, looking for their opportunity to steer me away from committed faith. The good news is, those doubts don't scare God. He is big enough to handle them.

One time I was speaking at a camp for high school students. At the end of the talk, I invited people to surrender wholly to Christ. Suddenly a hard-looking teen named Jake stood directly in front of me, staring at me intently. I saw pain in his eyes as he opened up to me: "I don't believe in the God you talk about," he said firmly. "My dad left me when I was a child. My mom's an alcoholic, and this church stuff doesn't work." I listened as he unloaded years of hardship.

Finally I interrupted him and did something I have never done before or since. I felt deeply impressed by the Spirit of God to ask Jake if I could pray for him.

"Why not?" He shrugged. He expected nothing but the same powerless, empty ritual he'd always known.

So I placed my hand on his shoulder and prayed one of the more daring prayers of my life: "God, Jake doesn't believe in You—but You believe in him. If You are real, please reveal Yourself to him at this moment."

Suddenly Jake started to tremble. His eyes widened. "God is on me! God is on me!"

I took a big step back…and just watched.

I'll never fully understand what happened just then. Moments before, Jake didn't believe in Him. But this callous, doubt-filled teen fell to his knees and cried out to God for mercy. Two years later, Jake contacted me to let me know that he had started his first job as a part-time youth minister.

Don't be afraid to ask the hard questions…but then do your homework. Study Scripture. Seek answers. Your pursuit will prove your faith.

SEALING DOUBT'S DOOM

Let's take one more look at our friend Thomas. He asked the questions. Then he sought the answers. The next part is the most exciting to me. Don't miss this. Jesus could have been angry about Thomas's doubt. When He appeared in that locked room to His disciples, Jesus could've chewed Thomas out. He could have publicly humiliated His so-called follower for his faith struggles. He could've put Thomas in a spiritual time-out.

Instead, Jesus, in His love and mercy, *gave Thomas exactly what his faith needed*: He invited Thomas to touch His risen body. Although we don't see Thomas taking Jesus up on His invitation, I don't think Jesus would have thought any less of him if he had.

I believe God will treat you with the same patient understanding. Ask the questions. Seek the truth. Then watch God give you what you need to help you believe.

God didn't straighten my crooked Jesus picture or move two sticks in the woods. That was what I *wanted*, to confirm my faith, but God gave me what I *needed*. He gave me His presence. It wasn't the tangible proof, but it was more real to me than any physical miracle. It was the reality of the presence of the One who died for me…and that is what my faith needed.

Sure, I've asked myself many times if that moment with God was real. Did one too many cheap Domino's pizzas give me indigestion dementia? Am I a few tacos short of a Mexican platter? You'll probably ask the same kinds of questions occasionally throughout your life. But God's presence—His goodness—continues to reassure me in the face of my recurring doubts.

And He'll do the same for you.

Jesus revealed himself to Thomas. The once-doubtful disciple responded, "My Lord and my God!" (John 20:28). Don't miss the power of this statement. Thomas believed *in* Jesus before. Afterward he *believed* Jesus. For a Jew to proclaim that Jesus was God was blasphemous, punishable by death, but Thomas didn't care…because he believed.

Thomas no longer dabbled in casual or convenient faith. After he asked the questions and sought the answers, Jesus gave him exactly what he needed to believe. Thomas reached his journey's goal—committed faith.

My own spiritual journey was marked by significant progress, followed by multiple setbacks. And at each point in the journey, God gave me what my faith needed. In seminary, it was the right professor. As a minister, it's been an answered prayer, a timely phone call from a friend, or the Bible verse that seemed to have been written just for me, just for what I was facing.

Take your doubts to God. He will provide what you need for committed faith.

SEVEN

I Feel Completely Inadequate

I feel *completely inadequate* to be a pastor.

There, I said it. But those words reveal only a brief glimpse of my insecurities. I also feel unqualified to be an author. And that's only the beginning of the list. I've also felt inadequate as a husband and a dad. Come to think of it, I've been insecure about almost every area of my life.

From the outside, it may look like I've got it all together. I'm leading a growing church, so I must be full of talent, creativity, and spiritual energy, right? I've had people compliment my leadership, my wisdom, and my preaching. But what they don't know is that I feel like a scared little boy hoping to make it through another week, and I feel that way...*all...the...time.*

I did well in school, but only by working my buns off. An intellectual giant I am not. I'm also pretty shy. Being with a lot of people makes me uncomfortable. No matter how hard

I try, I always seem to say something stupid. To top it off, I don't feel very spiritual. Don't get me wrong; I love God. But many people seem to love God so much more than I do.

So while people see me leading a large church, writing books, and speaking around the world, I live every day with the fear that I won't be able to pull it all off. I can't escape the feeling that certain failure is only one bad decision away.

I've been haunted with insecurities for as long as I can remember. And it's not just all in my head. I have concrete evidence proving my feelings of inadequacy. For example, the first funeral I officiated was a disaster. The deceased was a strong believer in her early nineties. Her death was a blessing: no more pain or suffering. She had gone to a much better place. It was a graveside ceremony, attended by a couple dozen people. All I had to do was show up, read some verses, say some nice words, and add a prayer—the epitome of a pastor's "easy" funeral.

And I managed to mess it up.

The granddaughter of the deceased wanted to sing "Amazing Grace." Nice idea. Wrong pastor. The problem? I can't carry a tune. But in front of the grieving family and friends, I attempted to sing the grand old hymn. Unfortunately (for me and everyone there), the small congregation thought the song was a solo. Even the granddaughter left me hanging. No one joined in. While I tortured a classic, I saw people looking at each other as if to say, *Why would a guy who sings so badly perform a solo?*

Several lines into the song, a fly came buzzing around my face. I was focusing all my attention on my first-ever—and last-ever—solo, when the fly zoomed straight into my mouth. (This sounds too crazy to be true. But believe me, I only *wish* I was kidding.)

Time froze, and I contemplated my options: *Should I hock a loogey and spit out the fly as discretely as possible in front of a grieving family? Or do I swallow a fly in the middle of "Amazing Grace"?* If anything in my life would ever qualify as a no-win situation, this was it.

Time unfroze. I decided to suffer for Jesus. I swallowed.

I couldn't imagine things getting any worse. Having just ingested a live winged insect, I ended the song early. I wanted to crawl into a hole and die. Then things got worse. After a short prayer, I was headed down the home stretch—ready to end the funeral with the "ashes to ashes" thing. Mustering my most authoritative pastor's voice, I started, "Ashes to ashes, dust to dust…" I hesitated. *Ashes to ashes, dust to dust…What comes next?* I couldn't remember.

That's when my train of thought derailed and wrecked— big time. *These people are sad*, I reasoned. *A little humor will do them good.*

The traditional funeral-finishing words that I had just spoken still echoed off the surrounding tombstones. *Ashes to ashes, dust to dust.* To them, I added the New Revised Groeschel ending: "I hope this coffin doesn't rust." Rare is the person who appreciates my sense of humor. And he wasn't at that funeral.

Did I mention that I feel completely inadequate?

INTELLECTUAL EXCLUSION

Some people come off as prideful—whether spiritually or in any other area of life. They believe they know it all. They live uprightly, and everyone else is wrong or morally inferior. These self-righteous, over-confident know-it-alls can be a real pain in the butt. (If you're a self-righteous, over-confident know-it-all, you just got mad because I wrote "butt." I did that just for you.)

However, more often than prideful people (who are generally just insecure people wearing a mask of pride), I see people fighting the same battle I fight—weighed down by deep feelings of inadequacy. While some may offer a résumé filled with victories in their faith, their family, their career... mine is overflowing with defeats, failures, self-doubts, fears, blunders, and insecurities.

Since I'm freely confessing, I'll tell you the main reasons I feel completely inadequate as a pastor. Maybe you'll identify with one or more of these.

First, *I don't feel I know enough*. I didn't become a Christian until I was in college. Before that I never read the Bible. For example, the Old Testament book of Job is supposed to be pronounced *jobe*. In a college Bible study, I shared that I'd been reading in Job. You can imagine my embarrassment when I realized people were giggling because I had pronounced it *jawb*. To this day, they still tease me for that.

You might wonder, *Didn't they teach you anything in seminary?* Which leads me to another confession: I graduated from seminary, but I wasn't paying attention. I was bored, uninterested, just jumping through hoops to get the degree.

I do work hard at learning the Bible. I read through it once every year, but it doesn't always stick. It's not uncommon for someone to ask something like, "Hey, Craig, do you remember the descendants of Zebulun in the book of Numbers?" And the whole time I'm thinking, *What's a Zebulun?*

I feel inadequate because I don't know enough. I'm guessing that is a fairly common struggle. As I was typing, one of my best friends just called. He's well-known for being a man of faith, with an awesome spiritual witness. My friend explained that he was asked to read a Scripture passage at his twenty-year high school reunion. He was nervous and wanted my advice. What Scripture should he read? My well-respected, spiritually mature friend doesn't feel he knows enough. So I'm reminded that I'm not alone.

But I still hate these feelings.

MORAL DISQUALIFICATION

I also think I'm inadequate because *I don't feel that I'm good enough.* A respectable pastor should be righteous. No bad words, no bad thoughts, no anger, no jealousy. Just faith, peace, and Christlikeness. When I look at Christians I respect—especially pastors—they seem to have it all together. They say the right things, behave the right way, and seem to have their spiritual act together.

Then there's me.

One of my most shameful moments involved a bad word—not just any bad word, but a really, really, *really* bad word. One day our basement flooded. The water was three feet deep (and rising), and many of our valuables were only moments from destruction. Frantically, I grabbed the power plug to my sump pump and waded into waist-deep water. Hanging from the rafter above was an extension cord. (You see where this is going?)

Standing waist-deep in water, I experienced a brief moment of insanity. I thought to myself, *If I plug this cord in REALLY QUICKLY, I won't get shocked.*

Idiot.

The moment the metal prongs touched live electricity, my body completed the circuit…to my serious displeasure. I wish that was the worst that happened. It wasn't. The worst part was the word that formed instinctively at the back of my head and traveled in a fraction of a second through my body—coordinating with the action of my lungs, my larynx, my tongue, and my lips—to bring it to ugly verbal reality.

I said a *big* one. A really big, bad word that preachers and other good people never say. (Which word? I'm willing to confess a lot, but I'll keep that detail to myself, thank you.) How can a preacher—one who explains God's love from his mouth—use the same mouth to utter such filth?

So much of the time I don't feel good enough.

BLUNDER BOUND

The third credential on my résumé for spiritual failure reads: *I've made too many mistakes.*

I've let you in on a lot of these sins already: the sex before marriage, the drinking, the lying. Heck, I cheated on every girl I dated except the one I married. And I've only told you the stuff I can print without freaking everyone out (and causing the hyper-spiritual Christians to slam the book shut and run, screaming, "Heretic!").

Most people would forgive the sins I committed *before* knowing Christ. So let's turn to my list of sins *after* Christ. At first glance, it may not look as bad, but upon closer examination, you might change your mind. Jealousy, envy, pride, doubt, a critical heart, gossip, ungodly competitiveness...and more. When I look at my current shortcomings, they reaffirm my earlier conclusion: I'm not good enough for God to use.

Maybe you feel the same way—too many doubts and not enough knowledge, too many sins and not enough forgiveness to get past them. Bad decisions can pile up to make a wall between you and what God wants you to do. But what we forget is God has enough grace and power to forgive every mistake and correct every flaw. If you're trapped by your inadequacies, maybe the stories of some insecure, blundering, sinful Bible characters will help you as they've helped me.

INCOMPETENTS WE LOVE

Which parts of the Bible encourage me most? They're the passages that tell about the men Jesus picked to be his disciples.

Notice first whom He did *not* pick. Of those chosen to carry the gospel to the world, Jesus didn't pick a single Pharisee, Sadducee, or scribe—the spiritual elite. Not one. Let that sink in for a moment. Jesus also didn't choose the best looking, the most talented, the best educated, or the most likely to succeed. Jesus chose twelve ordinary, sinful, insecure people—just like you. Just like me.

He chose a few fishermen, a tax collector, an accountant, and a political activist. Jesus nicknamed two of the guys "Sons of Thunder." This wasn't because they were born during a storm. Their reputations for wild living preceded them.

Jesus' friends were the most unlikely people to become disciples. They were the partiers of their day, the cheaters, the liars, the ones who the religious crowd despised. Jesus even hung around prostitutes. He surrounded Himself with the lowest, the poorest, the outcasts. And that encourages me.

So, what if you were valedictorian of your class, homecoming queen, or scored a 36 on your ACT? If you were the class president in high school, the star football player, or the best in the band, then I've got good news for you: God can still use you. It's just that He prefers to use those who are ordinary.

If, on the other hand, you feel like me—too stupid, too sinful, too mistake-prone…if you feel like you'll never measure up, that you don't have what it takes…if you feel like your best isn't good enough…embrace this: *God has prepared you to make a difference in this world.*

Still not convinced? Let me tell you about three more lives—fellow spiritual strugglers, deeply insecure. Allow their examples to encourage you toward kingdom greatness.

First, there's the prophet Isaiah. His life teaches us that *even if you've messed up big, God can still use you.*

After King Uzziah died, the whole nation of Israel panicked. While seeking God, Isaiah had a very unusual, life-changing vision. He saw the Lord, high and lifted up. Angelic beings bowed in worship, singing praises to the Holy One. After only a small glimpse of the holiness of God, Isaiah lamented, "Woe to me!... I am ruined! For I am a man of unclean lips, and I live among a people of unclean lips" (Isaiah 6:5).

Notice Isaiah's awareness of his own sin. *Woe to me.... I'm ruined.... I have unclean lips.* (Maybe he had a bad experience with a sump pump in his basement.) With this brief brush with our holy God, Isaiah became acutely aware of his impurity. He had messed up big. His unrighteousness stared him square in the face.

If you've ever felt too bad for God to use, you're in good company. Isaiah had sin on his lips. That's bad enough. But think of all the other substandard people God used. Sometimes the greatest were the ones who messed up the biggest. Moses murdered a man. Abraham was a liar. Jacob was a cheater. Rahab was a prostitute. David committed adultery. The apostle Paul even murdered Christians. And God used all these mess-ups to do awesome things.

I've already told you that I was an immoral, lying, deceiving, angry, thieving cheat. What about you? If you've messed up big, you're a leading candidate for God to use. So, what should you do now? Exactly what Isaiah did: Confess your sin. Let God cleanse and forgive you.

As Isaiah cried for mercy, a seraph touched the unclean prophet's lips with a live coal from the altar (where the lamb was sacrificed for sin) and said, "Your guilt is taken away and your sin atoned for" (v. 7). The moment after Isaiah experienced God's grace, the Lord asked the forgiven man, "Whom shall I send? And who will go for us?" Isaiah blurted out, "Here am I. Send me!" (v. 8).

And God did.

If you've messed up big—like me, like Isaiah—congratulations! You're at the top of God's talent-scouting list.

INEPT FOR THE GLORY OF GOD

How about another struggling Bible character? Let's take a look at Moses. When I think of Moses, I picture an amazingly courageous leader (who looks like Charlton Heston), full of determination to do God's will. But if you peel away his accomplishments and look at the real man, he doesn't seem so different from us. Moses' life teaches us that *God loves to use those who are unsure of themselves.*

God called Moses to lead His people out of bondage in Egypt. Then, to increase Moses' confidence in God's ability, God performed some really cool miracles. But instead of thinking about God's power, Moses was zeroed in on his own powerlessness. In response to God's call, the not-yet leader complained, "O Lord, I have never been eloquent, neither in the past nor since you have spoken to your servant. I am slow of speech and tongue" (Exodus 4:10).

In other words, *I hate public speaking. I stutter. Get a good speaker. Someone who loves to stand in front of large crowds. Count me out. I don't have what it takes.*

I get similar responses from people all the time. When I ask someone to lead a small group, their insecurities come out. *What if someone asks me something about the Bible that I don't know?* When I ask someone to lead a mission trip, timidity takes over. *But I wouldn't know how to lead a group that size. Can you get someone else?* When I ask someone to visit a sick person in the hospital, watch the backpedaling. *What if I say the wrong thing?* I have a hard time blaming them. I've been unsure of myself in almost every area of my life.

In 1994, my first daughter was born. To me, she looked perfect. But as a dad, I felt anything but perfect. *How do I feed a baby? Change a diaper? Doctor a rash? What will I do when she gets a fever? Skins her leg? Loses a tooth? What will I say when she can talk? And asks, "Who made God?" Will I tell her about the birds and the bees? What explanation will I offer when she discovers that people can be cruel? What if a boy breaks her heart, and I can't fix it? What if she marries someone I don't like?*

Just typing those old thoughts makes me sweat. I remember thinking, *I'll never be a good enough dad.* As hard as I've tried, even today I haven't shaken those feelings.

Years ago, when I was a timid, young pastor starting our church, a good friend, Dennis, told me something I'll never forget. After one of my days of particularly deep insecurity, Dennis sensed my struggle and boldly said, "God doesn't choose the prepared. He prepares the chosen."

I love that. You don't have to be ready for God to use

you. In fact, you might *never* feel ready. When God calls you, He'll prepare you with on-the-job training. With each step, He'll lead you. If you are unsure of yourself, you're in great company, and you're at the top of God's "Potential Disciples" list.

God spoke directly to Moses' greatest insecurity—fear of public speaking—by asking a series of probing questions: "Who gave man his mouth? Who makes him deaf or mute? Who gives him sight or makes him blind? Is it not I, the LORD? Now go; I will help you speak and teach you what to say" (vv. 11–12).

In other words, God will use you in spite of your insecurities. And He'll often use you where you're *most* insecure.

In what life skill do you feel weakest? Public speaking? Leading? Praying? Witnessing? Teaching? Forgiving? Parenting? God's grace is all you need. His power is made perfect in your weakness. (See 2 Corinthians 12:9.)

I've been teaching for years, and I'm still not a great Bible teacher. I never will be. I'm not that knowledgeable. I struggle with Greek. I'm still weak on biblical history. But I simply bring what I can. God brings the rest, and lives are changed.

One of my favorite aspects of preaching is what I call "the God factor." Regularly, people tell me that when I said "such-n-such," it changed their lives. The funny thing is, I didn't actually use the words they quote. God custom-designed a message for them. He took my weak words and personalized them by His Spirit. People heard what God was saying, not what I was saying.

And it works.

So do you feel unsure of yourself? Great. God can work more easily with insecurities than with pride. God is ready to use you. And, believe it or not, you're ready for His use.

HOPELESSLY USEFUL

A third biblical character who inspires me is David. His life teaches that *you are a candidate for God to use when others think you're not.* God loves to use the unlikely. When David was just a boy, God saw something in him that no one else saw.

God called the prophet Samuel to anoint the next king of Israel. So Samuel visited the Jesse household—a home with several likely candidates for king. The first was Eliab, the oldest. This guy had everything you'd expect a king to have: the looks, the physique, the brains. But God said to Samuel, "Do not consider his appearance or his height, for I have rejected him" (1 Samuel 16:7).

The proud, hopeful father, Jesse, paraded seven of his sons in front of Samuel. Each time God said no. Only one son remained. The runt. The baby. Jesse thought, *Him? The king? Ha! He won't qualify. God has already passed over all the mature, intelligent, and talented ones in the family.*

When Samuel asked if there were other sons, Jesse's reply

was drenched in doubt: "There is still the youngest…but he is tending the sheep" (v. 11). The Jesse family was about to learn that God loves to use people whom others believe are unqualified. As God told Samuel, "The LORD does not look at the things man looks at. Man looks at the outward appearance, but the LORD looks at the heart" (v. 7).

Then God chose the most unlikely—the youngest, the little shepherd boy, David. Why? Because God specializes in accomplishing His plans through unlikely people.

So what have others told you that you can't do? Be an effective teacher? Start a business? Raise great kids? Lead an organization? Get out of debt? Write a book? Lead a Bible study?

God uses the unlikely. He may do through you what others say can't be done. He loves to use people who others don't believe are ready. God has put more in you than those around you can see. And He looks past what the world looks for. God isn't searching for great looks, a full head of hair, the perfect figure, or the smartest or funniest person.

God is looking at what *He* put in you: quiet faith, untapped courage, dormant gifts. Others look at the outside. God sees *His* perfect work on the inside.

IDIOTS FOR CHRIST

So what do you do when you battle with feelings of deep inadequacy? I've learned to take my pastor's advice. He told me three things. First, *don't believe everything your fans say about you.*

Some believe you can do no wrong. Even though they love you, they'll never help you improve and will often tempt you in the wrong direction. Your friend may say you write better stories than John Grisham. Your new boss might say you'll be the company star in a year. "Don't believe all your positive press," my pastor would tell me. "You're not that good."

He also told me *not to believe everything my critics say about me.* My wise mentor promised, "The more you accomplish, the more you'll attract harsh criticism." Listening to constructive criticism is wise, to an extent, but anyone who focuses exclusively on negative press will eventually become defensive. God's people should remain on offense.

Get ready—the critics are coming. They won't like the way you parent, or how you drive, or the outfit you wore to the party. Don't focus on your detractors.

My pastor also reminded me that *the only opinion that matters is God's.* Listen to what *God* says about you. He believes in you.

One of my favorite verses in the Bible is Acts 4:13. Peter and John had been boldly preaching about Christ. Some of the legalistic, overly religious leaders had them arrested and questioned. Luke recorded their story: "When they saw the courage of Peter and John and realized that they were *unschooled, ordinary men,* they were astonished and they took note that *these men had been with Jesus*" (emphasis mine).

These were normal guys—just like you, just like me.

In fact, the Greek word for "ordinary" is the word *idiotes* (pronounced id-ee-AH-tace). It means "unskilled," and from it we get our word "idiot." Theses guys were like me—idiots! Not only were they *idiotes*, but they were also unschooled. I imagine they battled fears of not knowing enough. They probably felt intimidated in front of crowds. But...

These men had been *with Jesus*...and that made them extraordinary.

Don't listen to what anyone else says about you. Don't listen to the recorded tapes of negative words that your mind so easily accesses. Don't listen exclusively to either your fans or your critics. Instead, think about your whole life: your relationships, your finances, your ministry, your work, your witness, your influence. Spend time with Jesus, and let Him turn you from an ordinary person into an extraordinary disciple.

What is God calling you to do? "With Him," you can do it.

EIGHT

I Stink at Handling Criticism

I was traveling with my friend and fellow staff member Bobby to speak at a pastor's conference. After a short layover in Denver, we boarded for the final leg of the flight. I noticed a pastor friend of mine who was speaking at the same conference seated in first class. We exchanged hellos, and I headed to my seat in coach.

Later that evening, I bumped into him again. He expressed shock (and even seemed slightly offended) that I flew coach and not first class. He explained with all sincerity, "The man of God should travel comfortably. When you arrive to speak, you should be rested. You should always fly first class."

I chalked it up to a difference of opinion, but my friend wouldn't let the topic drop. He continued badgering me about all the reasons why pastors should fly in comfort. On and on he went, until finally I excused myself and walked away. I've been criticized for many things, but that was the first time I'd been criticized for not flying first class.

I completely respect his passion and motives. He's still my good friend (and will always be), but flying first class has never been my style. I don't travel enough to get free upgrades, and I personally don't see the added value that merits the enormous additional expense.

The next evening found Bobby and me on our way home. On the first leg of the flight, we sat in coach. While waiting in the Denver terminal for the second leg, Bobby noticed we were assigned to row one in first class. To this day, we don't know why were bumped up. Wow, we joked, God really has a sense of humor.

We enjoyed this little blessing...until we boarded the plane.

When the call came for first-class passengers to board, we felt slightly self-conscious, slipping onto the plane as unobtrusively as possible. A few moments later, the other passengers boarded, and, of course, they all shuffled right by us, two pastors "lounging in luxury."

The first guy we knew made a joke. "Must be nice sitting up here," he laughed as he passed.

The next acquaintance was a lady. She wasn't as nice. "It must feel great being an important pastor. The *regular* people have to sit at the back of the plane," she said sarcastically.

The third guy was downright rude. He'd apparently been

drinking, because his speech was slurred. To everyone within range, he shouted, "What a way to spend the church's money! Megachurch pastors live the megarich lifestyle."

First we were criticized for flying coach. Now we were criticized for flying first class, even though we never intended to. There are many ways to describe this kind of no-win situation. The nice way is: "Darned if I do and darned if I don't." Next time I'll just go sit in the john. Maybe there no one will criticize me.

On second thought, that might look even worse.

OPEN SEASON ON PASTORS... NO BAG LIMIT

The truth is, I stink at handling criticism—especially nit-picking, ignorance-based, selfishly motivated, unjustified criticism. I *should* be able to rise above it. I hate the way it always gets to me.

This confession reveals one of my greatest character flaws: I care too much about what people think. I should be consumed with pleasing God, but I'm often consumed with the impossible—trying to please people. I know it's wrong, but it's the truth. When people take their shots at me, I find myself wanting to defend my actions, justify my behavior, or even criticize back.

In the previous chapter, I admitted how inadequate I

feel. I think the more insecure we are, the harder it is to take criticism. Maybe that's why I have such a hard time ignoring harsh critiques: I'm already questioning myself, so having someone else find fault with me is pretty hard to take.

It's a little unlucky for me that tolerating critical people is part of a pastor's job description (article 7, paragraph 19.2, if you want to look it up). It's funny to me (if only I could laugh) how in the same week, the worship music can be both too loud and too soft, depending on which critic I'm speaking with. The auditorium can be too hot to one person and too cold to another. The insanely petty grievances go on and on. In a good week, the annoying complaints are relatively easy to dismiss. During more challenging weeks, the nonstop gripes are like water torture. They make me want to strangle someone (not literally, of course…).

Years ago, one church member's dog died of old age. Sugar, the fourteen-year-old mutt, went to wherever dogs go when they die. I'm very aware that for many people, their pets are a part of the family, and the loss can be traumatic. So I sent Sugar's human a card (the only card I've ever sent for the death of an animal), intending to follow up with a phone call. In my mind, I was displaying exceptional pastoral care.

To my shock, he called me first, extremely upset. At the top of his lungs he shouted, "HOW CAN YOU CALL YOURSELF A PASTOR? YOU…DIDN'T EVEN

VISIT ME IN MY HOME AFTER I LOST A FAMILY MEMBER!"

A house call for a dead dog? It never occurred to me.

YOUR LIFE IN THE FISH BOWL

I have a hard time accepting one of life's realities: Negative people simply won't go away. They've been around since the beginning of time. Even godly people in the Bible faced constant criticism. Moses married a foreigner, and for that, his siblings Aaron and Miriam criticized him sharply. The man who wrote two-thirds of the New Testament, the apostle Paul, was called a hypocrite and criticized for being a lousy speaker. Even Jesus Christ, the Messiah, took heat for healing on the Day of Rest, eating with the wrong crowd, and claiming to be the Son of God.

I'm sure you often face critical people. It could be your boss who's always breathing down your neck—whatever you do is somehow wrong. Maybe it's your parents—your clothes, hair, room, and attitude are all wrong. Or your spouse—you just don't measure up. You're criticized coming and going. You're just never good enough.

I battle two wrong desires when I'm criticized. Depending on the day, I'm tempted toward either *fight* or *flight*. Both responses are useless and wrong.

Most often, my first reaction is to fight, to defend myself, to silence my accusers. I feel bitter and I want to retaliate. Experience has taught me this method usually backfires. My fallback reaction comes when I'm fatigued from battle. When I don't feel like fighting, I resort to flight. I want to hide, to pretend that the criticism isn't real, to quit, to run away to another state, or stick my head in the sand.

God's method is better than either of these options.

In this chapter, I'll give you some useful strategies for dealing with critical people. It's never fun or easy, but it's necessary if you're going to make any sort of a difference in this world.

I learned a valuable principle about criticism from my mom. She always said simply, "Consider the source." In other words, before I focus too much on *what's* being said, I should ask myself *who's* saying it. The who is often more important than the what.

Why does that matter? Well, the *who* helps me determine my most appropriate response. Instead of fight or flight, the Bible provides three better responses: listen, answer, or dismiss. To choose the best of these three, we need to know who's offering the criticism, and why. What follows are a few pointers in the art of diagnosing, and dealing with, a critic.

Listen to criticism when it's appropriate. Proverbs 15:31–32 (NLT) says, "If you listen to constructive criticism, you will be at home among the wise. If you reject criticism, you only harm yourself." Some criticism is actually useful and important. Sometimes it's given from people who care enough about you to risk offending you. Their criticism is constructive. They offer suggestions to help you improve yourself. I try to listen to others when I believe their motives are pure.

My wife, Amy, constructively critiques me. She cares deeply about me and about my success in whatever I do. She's contributed more to my personal upgrades than anyone else. For example, after the first time I preached, she pointed out several things that I had done well. "You had great eye contact. Your passion was exceptional. You selected great Bible verses…and you looked great in those pants." (You're probably wondering if she really said that. Keep wondering.) Then she offered some helpful advice. "You kept putting your hand over your mouth. It made you look insecure and hesitant."

She was exactly right. And her advice made a big difference. When someone you love and trust offers advice, you're wise to take it to heart. Occasionally, someone outside your inner circle may offer constructive criticism. Outside criticism is hard to receive, but it may help you.

For example, I've been known to enjoy crude humor. I love Jesus and His standards of righteousness, but I still think a good potty joke is funny. I've even been known to share some of that kind of humor in my messages.

One time a group of three couples invited me to their house for a meeting. Because they cared deeply about me and our church, they wanted to help coach me through deep waters—deeper than I realized.

At the time, I had two small children. (Since then, my wife and I have gone the way of the proverbial bunny rabbits.) The three couples lovingly asked me how I would feel if my daughters grew up using potty humor. Through their gentleness and broader life experience, these couples helped me see the danger of my off-color wisecracks. They led me to become a godlier example and a more effective communicator.

It would've been very easy for me to write them off. *Who are they to correct me? Why should I listen to these old fogies, these stick-in-the-mud, legalistic fuddy-duddies? They wouldn't know a good joke if it jumped up out of their milquetoast bowl.*

But I would have missed the chance to grow.

Consider the source. If the source is a mature Christian—someone you can learn from—pay attention. When someone cares deeply for you, the Bible says you're wise to listen, even if the truth hurts. If you don't, you're only hurting yourself.

FILL IN THE BLANKS

Other times, someone may criticize you without the goal of helping—they simply want to voice dislike for you or something you've done. In some cases, you should *answer* the criticism.

When is it wisest to answer? Whenever you think that

offering a response can help the critic understand your position. But watch your attitude—simply answering can easily turn into defensiveness.

Consider answering critics when they're missing important information that could change their perception (and if you think they're open to listening). Maybe they only know part of the story. Perhaps tactfully providing one or two missing details could transform a critic into a supportive friend.

Gideon, one of Israel's national leaders, gave us a great model for answering criticism. The delegation from the tribe of Ephraim was upset that Gideon didn't seem to be paying them enough attention. Judges 8:1–2 recounts the story: "The Ephraimites asked Gideon, 'Why have you treated us like this?'... And they *criticized* him sharply. But he *answered them*..." (emphasis mine).

Gideon acted wisely. He gave them more information—in this case, information about the high regard in which he held them. He built up the Ephraimites with encouraging and positive words, and his answer helped them understand his heart and his thinking. "When the men of Ephraim heard Gideon's answer, they were no longer angry" (v. 3, NLT).

Sometimes a soft and wise answer can silence the critics. Try to choose an opportune time for your response. Think out your answer carefully, and prepare your heart to present your explanation in an appropriate way.

My wife and I are occasionally criticized for having six

kids. I usually explain that it's because I can't keep my wife off me. (Okay, maybe that's an exaggeration…) Also, our decision to home-educate our children sometimes draws criticism. But once we explain our reasons, many people soften their judgments. First, my wife has a degree in education. Second, we have a defined strategy for connecting our kids with other kids, to avoid isolation. Third, since I work almost all weekend, and many nights, if our kids were in public or private school, I'd rarely see them. Finally, we're confident God has led our family down this path.

Gentle, helpful answers sometimes make sense to the person with an open mind. If he or she is honestly seeking clarification or is simply confused, it's a pleasure to offer understanding. But if my critic is obviously not going to listen, I have to approach him in a different—and very difficult—way.

LIVING UPSTAIRS

Another appropriate response to invalid criticism may be simply to *dismiss* it.

I'm convinced that some people see only the bad side of everything. All of their silver linings have clouds. These horribly miserable individuals have the gift of dragging people down—especially themselves. I've chosen not to let them do that to me. If you face someone who can't be pleased, dismiss their invalid criticism.

Someone said that praise and criticism are windows to the heart. What a person praises and what he or she criticizes tells us a lot about that person. What we praise often reveals what we value most. If I say you have a beautiful car, chances are I value nice cars. If I tell you I'm impressed with your marriage, I probably value great relationships. If I go crazy over your yard, then I value a well-manicured lawn.

At the same time, the topics of our criticism often reveal our deepest insecurities. If I criticize you for being overly confident, chances are good that I have a self-esteem problem. If I judge you for living in a nice home, I may battle with materialism or jealousy. When dealing with overly critical people, try to see past the arrows to the struggles that launched them.

I've seen this truth play out dozens of times in ministry. The most striking example was a guy who threw a fit because his roommate was looking at pornography on his computer. With apparently righteous passion, Steve (not his real name) ranted about his roommate's lustful sins. He wanted to know if he should evict his roommate immediately. It took me several minutes to cool him down a few degrees. We prayed for his roommate, but when we hung up, Steve was still boiling about his friend's sin.

The next day I learned some tragic news. Steve had been having a three-year affair with a married woman. Steve's anger at his roommate was really a manifestation of his shame over his own transgression.

Perhaps that's why Jesus asked in Luke 6:41–42, "Why do you look at the speck of sawdust in your brother's eye and pay no attention to the plank in your own eye? How can you say to your brother, 'Brother, let me take the speck out of your eye,' when you yourself fail to see the plank in your own eye? You hypocrite, first take the plank out of your eye, and then you will see clearly to remove the speck from your brother's eye."

At one point in my life, I was dealing with a group of overly critical people. In the midst of the process, and unrelated to it, I had scheduled an early morning flight out of town. At 6:42 a.m., my plane lifted from the runway. Flying into the sunrise, the plane ascended higher and higher. When I looked out my window, everything on earth grew smaller… and I became more aware of just how big God is.

All of a sudden, in comparison to Him, my problems didn't seem so all-consuming. The plane's altitude served as a real-life metaphor illustrating my best response. With only a shift in outlook, I felt I had already risen above the problems.

Is someone picking you apart, finding fault with everything you do? Rise above the criticism. Let the wind of God's comforting, guiding Spirit lift you above the temporary problems. With His help, you can soar to new heights of maturity and confidence.

ANTAGONIST IN AGONY

It's especially helpful to understand who your critic is when he or she is emotionally unhealthy or wounded. It's a fact that "hurt people hurt people." They usually dislike themselves and criticize others in a misguided effort to validate themselves. If one of these injured souls lobs a criticism grenade in your direction, defuse it with understanding. Part of considering the source is seeking awareness of what that person may be going through.

Your critic may be struggling at work. He may be facing a midlife crisis. She may be several years into a painful marriage or weathering some other family problem. The person who just treated you rudely may have a dying parent or a sick child. Maybe you just got "lucky"—you were the closest target. Dismiss the criticism and love the person through their pain.

One time I was praying during worship, a few moments before preaching. Eyes closed, focusing on God, I felt someone slip a note into my hand. I never saw who it was, but the note was marked "Personal." I thought to myself, *Someone probably wrote a nice note to encourage me before I preach.* A warm, loving feeling settled over me as I unfolded the paper.

A moment later, I lost that loving feeling.

Evidently, the note was from a woman who had tried to see me on Friday, my day off. She took offense to my absence and blasted me with hateful accusations. This happened literally seconds before I was to stand up to preach. In that moment, I had a choice. I could internalize the offense and become demoralized and discouraged. Or I could ask myself, *I wonder what she's experiencing that caused her to lash out?*

I chose compassion over depression. My heart hurt for her. I knew that such a disproportionate reaction must indicate deep pain, so I didn't take her note personally.

Consider the source. And consider the possibility that the jab may come from an injured heart. Dismiss it and move on. If you don't, you may become the very thing you despise.

THE DRAGON IN THE MIRROR

I've always loathed critical hearts. Then one day I woke up and realized I was turning into what I hated—a snitty, cynical, sharp-tongued, nit-picking critic.

Talk about irony.

I could fault a person's diet, how they spent their money, how they walked and talked, and how they did or didn't perform their job. I was especially critical when it came to my area of passion—churches. I could walk into a church and tell the leaders everything they weren't doing right. Yet I recoiled in righteous indignation when someone else did the same thing to me.

Do you react as strongly to criticism as I do? Take a look

inside. You might find that you're a critical person yourself. If you are, you may not want to hear this, but I'm going to say it anyway: Let God deal with your heart.

Even if you have all the right answers and you know better than someone else, your "wisdom" will never change others for the better if it comes from a critical spirit. You're not helping anyone. You're certainly not helping yourself.

God convicted me, so I asked Him to change me. Now, years later, I can look back on a path of steady improvement. But the journey toward godlier thinking has not been an easy one.

I didn't grasp the depth of my disparaging nature until I decided to try to go a day without criticizing anyone or anything. I could barely make it fifteen minutes without a negative thought dominating my mind. My brain was conditioned to find fault. My hard drive needed to be reformatted.

So I made one of the best decisions of my life. If I couldn't stop the negative thoughts, at least I could stop the negative words. I committed to do just that. I won't tell you that I haven't failed, because I have...many times. But stemming the flow of critical words introduced my heart to positive change.

Once I began succeeding at stopping the bad, I made an additional commitment: I started looking for good. Wherever I found something praiseworthy, I'd talk about it. Instead of watching a church service and picking it to pieces, I'd talk about all the excellent ways God was using it. Suddenly I was amazed at all the good I could see. I removed my negativity lens, and my eyes opened to see God's work everywhere. Slowly my whole perspective changed. Now God uses me to help others improve—not by tearing them down, but by building them up. Ask Him to teach you to do the same, and see what a difference a little positivity can make.

DURABLE GOOD

Okay, sometimes you should listen to your critics. Sometimes you answer. And sometimes you dismiss.

But what if you can't ignore them? What do you do when people say things about you that are not true, and you try to dismiss them…but they resurface again and again and again? It's time to share a fourth response to criticism. I'm not going to pretend for a minute that it'll be easy.

When critical people just won't go away, I can only tell you one thing to do: *endure.*

Endurance is critical if you want to succeed spectacularly at anything God sets before you. Whenever you veer off the beaten path, whenever you blaze a new trail, you'll be criticized. Sometimes it will be relentless. You must endure.

In the church world, I'm grateful for the spiritual trailblazers. Ten of the twelve original disciples died a martyr's death spreading the gospel so that one day I'd hear and believe.

The church fathers of the first three centuries endured over-whelming persecution for their faith. Martin Luther faced a life-and-death trial for defending God's Word. Wesley, Finney, Moody, and Spurgeon patiently held up under criticism during the great historic revivals. Modern-day pioneers have endured battles to reshape and renew the church. Someone said you can always tell a pioneer by the arrows in his back.

I hope you're a pioneer. Maybe it's in business, in your family, in your faith, in medicine, or in missions. I pray God uses you to break new ground and make an eternal difference. However, when He does, you must brace yourself for more criticism and pain than you might imagine.

Are you facing a risky decision that could result in positive impact? Perhaps you fear the backlash of criticism or rejection. You cannot grow past your threshold for pain. Maybe it's time to face the pain and do the right thing.

Maybe you need to break up with someone you're dating. Perhaps you need to confront someone who's doing something wrong. Maybe you need to take a stand for righteousness at work, or take charge in your teenager's life. Your risk might be telling a loved one about Jesus. To succeed, you have to be able to suffer. And one of the most common pains obedient risk-takers face is the pain of criticism.

Jesus is our greatest model. He was willing to obey His Father's voice no matter what the cost. Hebrews 12:2 tells us to "fix our eyes on Jesus, the author and perfecter of our faith, who for the joy set before him endured the cross." It's for the joy and reward set before you that you endure the pain of risky obedience.

If God's calling you to do something, get to it. Fix your eyes on Jesus. Be obedient. For the joy set before you, endure your unavoidable opponents.

HANG ON TO YOUR HALL PASS

Listen. Answer. Dismiss. Harder still, endure.

Above all else, never forget: *You can't please all people, but you can please God.*

No matter how hard you try, you'll never please everyone. It's an impossible goal. Give up trying to please the unpleasable, and live first of all for God, your Father, who always has a smile ready for you. I love the way Paul says it in 1 Thessalonians 2:4: "Our purpose is to please God, not people" (NLT).

If, like me, you hate being criticized, recognize that the root problem is that we're people pleasers. Once we find freedom from our need for people's approval, we can focus on the eternal goal of bringing pleasure to God.

How do we shake the desire to satisfy every human? The answer's simple: Know who you are *in Christ*. In Christ we are forgiven. In Christ we are secure. In Christ we are free.

You are who God says you are, not who people say you

are. Don't try to base your life on the unstable foundation of human opinions, but instead, build on the unshakable truth of God.

Let me approach this from a different direction. When I was in grade school, I lived for the privilege of performing the most honored tasks. One of my greatest thrills was to be the one who turned the lights off before the teacher started a video. Another was—are you ready for this?—to actually *turn on* the video. (Exciting childhood, huh?) The highest privilege, though, was to run an errand for the teacher...*in the hall*. Now that was living!

If the teacher happened to pick me for the errand, my heart would beat faster with anticipation. I approached her desk worshipfully. My mission was outlined, and then she gave me...(drumroll, please)...the hall pass.

Armed with the hall pass, the World of the Halls was suddenly opened to me. I explored otherwise inaccessible territory with confidence. If any teacher stopped me and asked what I was doing out of class, I'd whip out my hall pass. If someone wondered where I was going, I'd show them my hall pass. That precious piece of paper, signed by my teacher, meant I was completely secure.

The Bible is your hall pass, signed by God.

If you've trusted Christ as your Savior, the Bible tells you who you are "in Him." No matter what anyone else thinks, you're forgiven, free, and secure. When someone says, "You're not good enough. You don't measure up. You made a stu-pid decision. I don't like your leadership. You don't belong here"—whip out your hall pass, God's Word. The truth.

The truth is your high ground. The truth is your 747, soaring above the clouds. When you cling to the truth, you can rise above the criticism.

NINE

I'm Afraid
of Failure

It drives me...twenty-four hours a day, seven days a week, 365 days a year. It never takes time off. It never sleeps. It consumes me—God's sworn enemy: fear.

I've already told you about my worries and fears. Now I want to introduce my one monster fear, the one that seems almost impossible to escape...

Failure.

What if I fail leading the church, and I disgrace the name of Christ? What if the church struggles financially, and staff families who trust me suffer? What if I push too hard and burn out? What if I give everything, but that's not enough?

Fear of failure haunts me daily.

Bill Hybels, a pastor and friend of mine, once spoke with a leading national military official. This war hero described for Bill intense life-and-death decisions in battle. Bill listened respectfully, but inwardly thought, *I wish my issues were simply life and death. I deal daily with* eternal *life and* eternal *death.*

That's my responsibility, too. Imagine the consequences of my failure: *What if my preaching doesn't reach the lost? What if I make a bad decision and turn thousands away from Christ? What if passionately building a church costs me my family?*

Whether or not you're a pastor, the charge of sharing your faith can put the fear of failure in you: *What if I say the wrong thing to this nonbeliever, and he never knows God because of me?* Or maybe you have children, and you're afraid they'll go astray, that you'll fail as a parent. Whatever our responsibilities are, if we take them seriously, we don't want to fail, and if we allow ourselves, we can live daily in fear of our next misstep.

As you read this, I pray that God will help you see in yourself any fear of failure and that He'll guide you to confront that fear head-on. If you do, you'll be able to do things you always thought were impossible—believing they were too risky. You could start a business or a family. You could go into full-time ministry. You might volunteer to lead a Bible study. Or perhaps retire early, offering your gifts to a nonprofit group. Or maybe you'd ask out that person you've been staring at in class for two semesters.

If you stop submitting to your fear of failure and start obeying God, you'll never be the same. But I promise you, your spiritual enemy will do everything in his dark power to scare you away from God's best. That's why you have to start learning to see failure God's way.

FAILSAFE

Reflecting on my earliest childhood memories, fear of failure intimidated me from the beginning. *What if I don't make an A? What if the cute girl in the eighth grade won't go to the dance with me? What if I run for class secretary and lose? What if I don't make the soccer team? What if I can't get into the college I want?*

What if I fail?

My dad played minor-league professional baseball, so sports have always been a big part of my family's life. Before I graduated from training wheels, I was throwing fastballs off a homemade pitcher's mound in our backyard. I was born and bred for the sport.

But baseball's always bothered me. Why? Because I hated striking out. Or grounding out. Or popping out. Or making an error. Baseball is a great sport—unless you don't like to fail.

In the eighth grade, a pitch hit me, breaking some fingers on my throwing hand. After that, fear paralyzed me—I couldn't hit. *What if I got nailed by an eighty-mile-an-hour fastball? What if I broke my whole hand? Or got beaned in the head?* Instead of facing my fears, I quit. That's exactly what most people do. It looks safe, but it's actually very costly.

Jesus illustrated the fear of failure in Matthew 25, where He talked about a wealthy man who entrusted his money to three servants to invest on his behalf. When the man checked up on his servants, one of them said, "Master…I knew that you are a hard man…. *So I was afraid* and went out and *hid your talent in the ground.* See, here is what belongs to you" (vv. 24–25, emphasis mine).

Did the master commend such cautious discretion? No! He was a businessman. He shouted, "You wicked, lazy servant!" Then he took the money away from the fearful servant and gave it to another servant, one who had risked his money and multiplied it (vv. 26, 28).

What motivated the unfaithful servant? Fear of failure. Because of it, he avoided risk by burying his master's money. How many people do that today? Instead of trying something new, many stay at home. Rather than accepting an invitation to make a difference, lots of Christ followers "play it safe."

What are you afraid of? Are you avoiding asking for a raise, afraid you might not get it? Is there a job you know you'd love, but you're afraid of rejection? Are you afraid of intimacy, fearing you might get hurt again? Do you avoid having children because you might not be a good parent? Is your fear of failure holding you back? We've forgotten that the most dangerous thing we can do…*is play it safe.*

That's what the unfaithful servant did: hedged his bet, avoided his fears…and buried his master's money. His decision forfeited any future opportunity to make a difference for his master.

What if Jesus took your opportunities—or mine—and gave them to someone else?

FAILURE BY THE NUMBERS

Scientists once conducted a very illuminating experiment. In the middle of a room, they hung a bushel of fresh bananas halfway up a pole. Then they let four monkeys loose in the room. Immediately the hungry monkeys dashed toward the bright yellow bananas. As they climbed the pole, one of the scientists blasted the monkeys with icy-cold water.

The monkeys backed off, regrouped, then made a second attempt. As they started to climb the pole, once again they received the discouraging dousing. After several unsuccessful attempts, the monkeys became convinced that failure was inevitable and finally stopped trying.

The next day, the researchers removed one of the four monkeys and replaced him with a new monkey. What did the rookie do? He went straight for the bananas. But before he even reached the pole, the three veterans pulled him away. Undeterred, the new monkey tried again. Again his compassionate roommates intervened. At last he gave up and adopted their fatalistic attitude.

Each day, the scientists replaced one of the original

monkeys with a new one. By the fifth day, four monkeys occupied the room, none of whom had ever been sprayed with cold water. From that day forward, whenever a new monkey was traded in, the others would prevent him from going for the bananas...*without even knowing why*. Four had failed, and then they conditioned the novices to not even try.

That happens a lot in life, doesn't it? Someone gets hurt in a relationship and tells everyone else, "Don't risk the pain. Stay single." Someone wounded by a Christian spreads the word: "Christians are hypocrites. Don't trust them." A teenager makes some bad decisions, and his parents advise a younger couple, "Don't have kids. They'll wreck your lives." To avoid potential failure and pain, people abort their dreams. They stop trying.

Don't let fear of failure make a monkey out of you.

(Sorry about that. I couldn't resist.)

FATED TO FAIL

Your spiritual enemy wants to steal, kill, and destroy God's purpose in your life (see John 10:10). That's what he does, and fear is one of his favorite weapons. But the apostle Paul said, "God has not given us a spirit of fear" (2 Timothy 1:7, NKJV).

Fear of failure doesn't come from God. It's time to face it. I'm ready to face my fear of failure. Will you? Ready? Great! You go first. *Just kidding.* Let's tackle this ogre together...

The way to beat fear of failure is to learn and internalize *God's Philosophy of Failure*. It includes several components, which I'll explain. As they unfold, you'll see that they pave the pathway to freedom. Your first step on the path is...

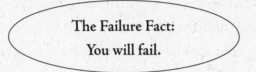

The Failure Fact:
You will fail.

Can you feel the freedom already? What? No?

You're right—this seems like a strange way to begin a journey to freedom. This first fact of God's Philosophy of Failure doesn't sound encouraging. It doesn't even sound pleasant. But it's essential that you grasp this truth if you want to defeat the destructive fear of failure.

Failing is a part of life. In fact, it's often one of the most important ingredients in the stew of success. *You will fail.* The Bible says, "We all stumble in many ways" (James 3:2). All of us stumble...and fail. Not just in *some* ways, but according to James, in *many* ways. It's a part of growing and becoming all that God wants us to become. If we avoid attempting to succeed, we'll most likely fail even bigger than if we had tried. Did you catch that? If your concern is to avoid losing, *the best way to cut your losses is to take good risks.*

Because of my fear of failing, I avoided preaching or teaching the Bible for years. If someone invited me to teach a Bible study, I'd politely decline. Why? I didn't want to fail.

But one day my pastor, Nick, invited me into his office. I could tell he was serious when he said, "I don't trust very many people to preach for me. But I think you're ready. What do you say?"

My heart skipped a beat. I said shakily, "I guess I'm ready," but I didn't believe it.

My pastor smiled broadly, ignoring my obvious timidity, and responded, "Great! You're on this Sunday."

I almost passed out.

I wish I could tell you I faced the fear, prepared a great message under God's clear direction, and stepped boldly to the pulpit to preach. I'd like to report that the Spirit of God empowered me, that I did an awesome job and changed hundreds of lives.... Nothing like that happened. Instead, I agonized for three days, unable to choose a text or topic. Nick ended up preparing most of the message for me. The night before, I didn't sleep a wink.

Sunday morning, I rolled out of bed, exhausted, and put on my only suit. Even after five attempts, I couldn't get my tie right. I shined my shoes and went back over my notes. Then I drove to the church—where I promptly commenced vomiting.

When I stood up to preach, my face blotched horribly. People in the crowd glanced at each other nervously. Surely someone so young couldn't be having a stroke. My heart pounded. My throat went dry. I could barely speak. Finally, after the first several awkward minutes, my throat cleared, and my words became moderately intelligible. My confidence grew.

"God knew you before you were even born," I preached.

A few people, hoping to help me along, said, "Amen."

"God knew you before your mommy knew your daddy," I said, even bolder.

More polite amens.

Then I boomed passionately, "God knew you before you were an itch in your daddy's pants!"

No amens. Only groans. Shudders. A few of the teenagers giggled.

Everyone fails. You will. I will. It's a part of growing, a part of life.

NOTHING PERSONAL

After that Sunday's service, Nick wrapped his arm around me and said with a fatherly smile, "Well, no one will forget your first sermon!"

I can laugh about it now, but at the time, I was absolutely crushed. I faced my fear of failure…and lost. The risk didn't pay off (I thought). I failed—miserably. Many pastors wouldn't have given me a second chance. I'm so thankful I had one who did. Nick continued to believe in me. He offered me a life-changing concept. I wish I could remember it word-for-word, but it went something like this:

"Everyone fails. I'm not going to lie to you and tell you that you didn't. Feel the disappointment. It'll make you determined never to fail in the same way again. Don't buy into Satan's lies of *disapproval*. That's a different matter. Your enemy will try to bury you under your disappointments. Remember, Craig, *just because you failed at something, doesn't mean you're a failure.*"

Then he shared with me another component of God's Philosophy of Failure. I had always taken failure very personally. I believed that I, myself, was a failure. This wasn't true. Now I understand…

The Failure Fallacy Reframed:
Failure is an event, never a person.

Think about those words. I pray they speak to you as they did to me.

I've known people whose greatest dream was to honor God with their marriage. Then they woke up one day, divorced, hearts broken, dreams shattered.

If that's you, *you are not a failure.*

I've known others whose world came crashing down under financial disaster. Many have filed for bankruptcy, feeling that temporary setback will doom them for the rest of their lives.

If you've experienced that valley, *you are not a failure.*

Others have lost jobs. Made poor child-raising decisions.

Taken bad advice. Dropped out of school. Fallen into sin. There's no end to the list of ways we can fail.

These people are not failures...and neither are you.

THE FRUIT OF THE FLUB

I'll always be grateful that Nick took the time to start filling out my understanding of God's Philosophy of Failure. I'm also glad that, years later, he took me to the next step. Nick and I were reflecting on that first failed attempt at preaching. As we came down from a long bout of laughter, he said something I'll never forget:

"I can't prove it, but I think God wanted you to fail on your first try."

What?! I wanted to shout. *How could God* want *me to fail?* The idea went against everything I wanted to believe about God.

Nick explained...

Failure's Function:
God often accomplishes good
results through failure.

"You learned a lot more through your mistakes than you would have learned through succeeding," Nick said.

I didn't want to admit it, but he may have been right.

God worked in me through my failures. What did I learn?

I learned humility. I learned dependence on God. I learned to pick myself up, get back on the horse, and face my fears. I learned to study harder, pray more, and allow God to prepare my heart. I started putting more confidence in His presence than in my abilities. Most importantly, I learned that failure is only temporary. In many ways, I'm a better man today because of my early failures. As I reflect on my life, almost every success followed a failure. Without a doubt, I've learned more from the "losses" than I have from the "wins."

What if God allows you to fail at something? While you lament a wrecked relationship, ask God what He wants to teach you. Rather than hating yourself because you said the wrong thing, maybe you can learn what you should say next time. Instead of sinking into depression when you fall, maybe you can get up, taking a new stand with greater wisdom and determination.

Everyone fails, but failures aren't permanent—unless we refuse to learn from our mistakes.

THE FORCE GREATER THAN FAILURE

Now, it's true that you need failure in order to grow. Does that mean failure is, in every respect, your friend? No. Failure is an obstacle, an enemy to overcome. We grow from failure through the lifelong experience of learning to defeat it.

You can't win by yourself. Failure is a giant you *will*

conquer on your way to success, but not alone. You have to remember...

> **The Failure-Fighting Fellowship:**
> **With God, you can overcome failure.**

Proverbs 24:16 says, "Though a righteous man falls seven times, he rises again." Throughout Scripture, the righteous man (or woman) is the one who lives depending upon God.

If you fall, with God's help, you can get back up. If you fall a second time, He'll help you up again. Three times? He's still there, and you can do it again. And again. And again. And again. (Seven times isn't literal—this promise never expires.)

Think about a *Rocky* movie (any of them—*Rocky I* or *II* or *III*...or *XXXVIII*). Being knocked down doesn't mean you're knocked out. You can always get up and fight again—because you're tag teaming with the Masked Maker. In fact, I would go so far as to say that there are some things you can't see until you look at them from the perspective of failure.

That's why I believe that another component of God's Philosophy of Failure is...

> **Failure Facing Forward:**
> **Failure is often the price you**
> **pay for progress.**

During seasons of failure, God is shaping us. If we take a risk, we might not succeed, but if we avoid all risk, we *guarantee* we won't succeed, and we miss so much of what God wants us to learn.

Some people think everything we've tried at my church has worked. Nope. In fact, most of what we've tried hasn't worked. We've only been able to pioneer so many successful ministry innovations because we've learned from dozens—even hundreds—of failures.

As of this writing, our church meets in nine locations and has thirty-seven weekend worship experiences. I teach five times on a typical weekend, and the other thirty-one worship experiences receive my teaching via live satellite video. Because this works so well, most people assume that video teaching has always worked for us.

They've never heard of Avodah. *What? Video avocados?*

Uh…no. Let me explain. Avodah was our first attempt at a video worship experience. It's now extinct. In less than six months, it failed miserably. Died. Buried, deep, deep underground. I guarantee it will never rise from its grave (the location of which is a national security secret).

After that discouraging early effort, we might easily have thought, *Video teaching will never work. We tried and failed. Why try again?* But from that experience, we learned how to select and develop the appropriate leaders. We learned about who we are as a church—and who we're not. We learned where to better invest resources, and where not to waste them. We learned about promotion, about caring for people personally, and how best to work with teams. Our thirty-one successful video experiences cost us the price of the first failed one. Failure is often the price you pay for progress.

Are you struggling against failure right now? Does a recent failure linger painfully in your memory? You thought you were creating the next Mercedes, but you got a Pinto. What do you do now?

Look for what God's teaching you. What's happening *to* you is not as important as what God's doing *in* you. Maybe He's shaving off some pride, or teaching you to depend on Him, or building some undeveloped character trait. Look past the painful outward circumstances and embrace God's inner artistry. Whatever you do, don't give up. If you hang in there, you'll eventually succeed *God's way* and on *God's timetable* (see Galatians 6:9).

So you've been knocked down. Get up. Again. And again. Learn and move on. You'll face another fight tomorrow—and when you do, you'll be stronger and wiser than you were today.

ALWAYS GO OUT,
BUT NEVER WITHOUT IT

Well, Craig, I see your point. But I'm going to take my chances on not taking any chances. Won't God be happy with whatever I can do for Him within the safe boundaries of my own choosing?

In a word…no!

If you've placed your faith in Christ, then God is your Father, and He'll never reject you. But that doesn't mean He's always happy with your behavior as His child. The only way to please God is to open yourself up to…

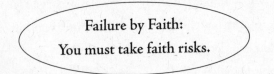

**Failure by Faith:
You must take faith risks.**

You can't please God by giving in to complacency and comfort.

Oh yeah, Groeschel? Prove it!

Okay. Here's what God says: "Without faith it is impossible to please God" (Hebrews 11:6). In other words, you *cannot* play it safe and please God. It's impossible.

I can't, either, but I've sure tried! I've lived most of my life trying to eliminate risks. I wouldn't ask a girl out unless I had assurance she would say yes. I wouldn't interview for a job unless I had a good chance of getting it. I avoided classes in college that would've stretched me.

Some settle for less than their ideal marriage partner. Others seek only lackluster careers. Many have dreams, but never act. Instead, they play it safe, longing for comfort and striving for guarantees of a trouble-free life—"guarantees" that are null and void from the start.

Don't avoid risks. Take the *right* risks. When was the last time you took a faith-risk? When have you believed God was calling you to do something you couldn't do on your own? When have you pulled away from the shore and launched into the deep?

I once met with some leaders from one of the largest, best known churches in America. This church is successful now because of many early risks. For years, these pioneers attempted feats that had never been accomplished before.

At the time of our meeting, that was all in the history books. I made a suggestion that could've taken this church to a level of effectiveness that few churches in the world have achieved. The leaders gasped, shocked. Then they relaxed and chuckled. "That would be too big of a risk," said one spokesman.

"But your church was built on risks," I countered.

"Yes, Craig," the spokesman said, trying not to sound condescending, "but when you reach our size, you'll realize you can't take that kind of risk."

I wanted to scream, "NO!" But I could understand their fear. I know it all too well.

Maybe you feel the same way. Your excuses are worded differently, but they come from the same source:

At this point in my life…

If you were my age, you'd understand…

Given my health…

In my financial condition…

The reasons we "can't afford" to take risks are infinite.

If you think this way, you have to ask yourself: How can I possibly please God? Faith is believing in what you can't see, following a voice you can't prove you heard, and living by principles that God says are true but don't make sense in this world. Without faith, you cannot please God.

I told my executive staff members how, once, I had risked so much to start the church…how I then took even more risks by hiring them (I was only joking, of course). Then risked even more by adding a second campus. Then took risks with experimental video teaching. I proudly rattled off my résumé of accomplishments—all the times I'd faced and defeated my greatest fears.

Suddenly one staff member interrupted and asked respectfully, "What big faith risk have you taken in the last two years?"

Silence.

I had to admit that I hadn't taken any. Without realizing it, I had slouched into the habit of basking comfortably in the glory of yesterday's success. For some time, I had sailed the tranquil sea of complacency.

That night, I came home deeply unsettled, my mind whirling. Our bedroom was dark, and as I walked through it, I was startled to see a small, human-shaped object flying in my direction. Instinctively, I prepared to take my attacker down. Also in that instant, I identified the UFO as my seven-year-old daughter, airborne. Her stomach landed awkwardly on my head. I managed to catch her, and we tumbled to the ground.

I was dazed. She laughed uproariously.

"What were you thinking?" I asked, still winded.

"I waited here for you in the dark for about a half hour and decided to jump on you when you came in."

"Why?" (The wisdom of a seven-year-old's logic escapes me.) She didn't say *duhhhh*, but her tone implied the stupidity of my question. What she *did* say, with exasperation, was, "Daaaaddddyyyy, because I just knnneeeewww you would catch me."

Oh.

Childlike faith: Daddy would catch her if she jumped. So, with that lesson in mind, I started listening for my heavenly Father's voice. Next time He told me to jump, I had to trust that He would catch me.

Do you remember the story about Jesus' disciples riding in a boat during a storm? Jesus wasn't with them, and they were freaking out. (Which is exactly what I'd be doing, riding in a small, rickety fishing boat during the Perfect Storm.) That's when Jesus miraculously walked toward them on the water. Then the disciples *really* started to wig out, thinking Jesus was a ghost.

Trying to calm them, Jesus said, "Take courage, it is I" (Matthew 14:27).

Then one disciple spoke up. Above the terrified shouts of the others, Peter said, "Lord, if it's you, tell me to come to you on the water" (v. 28).

Jesus responded with one word: "Come" (v. 29).

Is Jesus saying that to you?

Come. Follow Me.

Come. Let Me lead you.

Come. Leave your comfort behind.

Come. Trust Me.

The next line of Matthew's story will always amaze me: "Then Peter got down out of the boat, walked on the water and came toward Jesus" (v. 29).

Would you have done what Peter did? Eleven other disciples didn't. Even though they had seen the same miracles and spent time with the same Jesus, they stayed in the boat. I can't tell you why they wouldn't hop onto the choppy, icy water. But I know why I wouldn't. I'd be afraid I'd sink. In other words, I'd cower in fear of failure. Again.

Why did Peter do it? Because he suddenly grasped—even if only for a moment—the basic principle of God's Philosophy of Failure, the bedrock for all the rest of this chapter's teachings. Namely...

The Unfailing Father:
God never fails.

How can you become firmly convinced of God's absolute trustworthiness? Peter's courageous move shows us the only way: You have to step out to find out. You'll never know what God can do through you until you leap over the gunwale and get your feet wet.

ACHE OF THE UNCROSSED CHASM

So what are you waiting for? Fear of failure is natural for those of us who don't like pain. But if you haven't noticed by now, one of life's greatest pains is…regret. If you don't face your fear, climb your mountain, cross your ocean, one day you'll wake up and voice one of the most excruciating statements of your life—the words of regret:

I wish I would have…

I wonder what would have happened if…

I always thought I was supposed to…but I never tried.

I always thought I'd have time for…but now it's too late.

If you don't confront and subdue your fear of failure, you'll certainly live with the pain of regret.

I'm closing my laptop after I finish these last few lines. I have a risk I have to take. There's someone I need to call—a relationship that needs healing. Sure, I fear failure, but I'm going to feel the fear…and do what God's calling me to do anyway.

How about you? Ready to face your fear?

I'll go first.

(Closing the laptop.)

TEN

One Last Confession

The week I found the *Playboy* at the airport, I told our whole church about the experience. That same week it also happened that Maggie attended one of our small groups. It was her very first time.

Maggie was an exotic dancer—living behind a wall of lies. No one in this small group knew about her occupation. And as much as she hated her lifestyle, she didn't know how to escape it.

During the group's discussion, one of the guys, Trevor, said he needed to talk. Voice trembling, Trevor began a confession of his own. "Since Pastor Craig was daring enough to talk to the church about his struggles, I'm going to open up to you. I have a lust problem, and I look at pornography every day."

No one in the group flinched or dropped a jaw. They simply listened, lovingly, without judgment. Full of grace and acceptance.

When Trevor finished, the group embraced him and prayed for him on the spot. That's when first-time guest Maggie burst into tears. Once she regained her composure, she explained that she had never experienced unconditional love like she had just seen. No one yelled at Trevor or called him a spiritual loser. No one condemned him or beat him down. Instead, the group accepted him, demonstrating God's love.

It was time for her to tell her story.

Through sobs, Maggie revealed her darkest secret to her new Christ-following friends. She wanted out of exotic dancing, but she felt trapped. The pay was good, and as a single mom, she couldn't afford to quit.

Suddenly Trevor blurted out, "Maggie, if you quit your job tomorrow, this group will cover you financially." Everyone else agreed and offered their full support.

Maggie sat stunned. *How could this be? How could anyone be so loving? So generous? So full of grace?*

Moments after revealing her most embarrassing secret, Maggie collided head-on with the love of Christ shown through His people.

On Monday, Maggie quit her old job. On Wednesday, a girl from our group helped her land a new one. Today Maggie helps other girls escape from the exotic-dancing industry.

All because she took a risk. She was tired of hiding, of pretending, of living a lie.

So was I on that Sunday not so many years ago.

That's why I wrote *Dare to Drop the Pose*. Because keeping up appearances was preventing me from telling the truth and—even more importantly—from making long-overdue personal changes. Once I started coming clean, I realized that authenticity as a way of life has huge payoffs. And I never want to go back.

My one last confession?

I confess that what I wanted *most* to happen when I wrote this book was that you, too, would join me in a taking the risk: to drop the pose, choose honesty, and get real with God as a way of life.

God is calling you and empowering you to live an authentic life, to have courage, to be genuine. Colossians 3:9–10 reminds us, "Do not lie to each other, since you have taken off your old self with its practices and have put on the new self, which is being renewed in knowledge in the image of its Creator."

The old, pretend self is gone. If you will let Him, God will renew you—in His image.

Of course, the easiest thing for any of us to do when we're confronted with change is to just keep doing what we've always done. But the fact is, getting real isn't just what we *could* or *should* do—it's what we *must* do if we're going to experience the life that Jesus promises.

When *they* chose to change, Trevor and Maggie set in motion a sequence of positive results that surprised them, started them on a fresh new life, and blessed others around them. God is ready to set off the same sequence of transformation in your life, too.

I invite you to join me in a radical commitment to live the most authentic, transparent, vulnerable life a Christ follower can. Once you do, you'll find as I have that even though some people might not like you as much, the ones who do like you will like you a *lot* more. For once, people who matter to you will be able to know and love the real you.

And finally, you'll be set free to love them back.

It has been my honor to share my real self with you.

Now it's time for you to put the book down and make your own choice. I say, go with the real thing.

CONVERSATIONS:

A Study Guide for Personal or Group Use

INTRODUCTION
I HAD BEEN LIVING A LIE

Big Idea: "Over a lifetime a well-intentioned follower of Jesus can succeed at building an impressive exterior but fail miserably at being the real thing—the person God so lovingly created in the first place," writes Craig. The personal loss of becoming a pretender is huge, but fortunately we don't have to live that way. A dedication to honesty, authenticity, and vulnerability can, with God's help, set us on the path to a life of freedom, genuine relationships, and lasting blessing.

1. What were you feeling as you read Craig's story— Anxious? Guilty? Angry? Hopeful? Where do you think those feelings were coming from?
2. Craig admits, "You may not like me after reading this book." Well, what would you tell him now that you've heard his confessions?

3. Have you ever gone through a difficult season when you've wondered if a "real you" even existed? Talk about what that felt like and what might have been prompting your personal crisis.

4. Do you think smart, outgoing people struggle more with being real? Or average, shy ones? Or do you think being real is a human problem we all deal with in different ways?

5. Have you ever played games with God where, for example, you think you're fooling Him (go figure) about your actual motives or feelings? Talk about that experience.

6. Have you ever found yourself confessing something painful and unlikable about yourself in public? To someone else whose opinion really matters to you? If so, describe what was going through your mind before, during, and after that experience. Did good things come to you and others from that experience, or not?

7. Would you say you sincerely want a life "free of fear... and secrets...and doubts...and insecurities," like Craig writes about? If so, how far are you willing to venture in faith to make it happen? How motivated do you think God might be to help you?

CHAPTER 1
I CAN'T STAND A LOT OF CHRISTIANS

Big Idea: You expect it to be otherwise, but sometimes Christians can be the most difficult people! They can be judgmental, narrow-minded, phony, stingy, and self-righteous. But, as Craig admits, the least appealing faults are the ones we see in ourselves. We long to be so much more and better than we are. What should we do? We must ask God to change our motivations *and* our actions to be more like Christ. He asks us to be set apart, pure, selfless, committed to showing His love to the lost, and (this is where it gets hard) committed to loving the people of God.

1. What kind or kinds of people tend to irritate you the most? How do you usually respond?
2. Which behaviors or attitudes that are common among followers of Christ bother or embarrass you the most? Why do you think some Christians think or act in these ways?
3. Is it wrong to expect more of Christians than of non-Christians? Explain your answer.
4. Would you say you're more critical of others or more critical of yourself? Why or why not?
5. If an objective observer evaluated your thoughts, your giving, and your serving, would he or she come to the conclusion that you are a follower of Christ?

6. In what areas have you most often asked God to help you change? Do you see any progress?

7. Craig writes: "Before I was a pastor, I used to think that church should serve me, until I let God change my attitude. I was a taker, not a giver. I wanted a church that would provide what I needed. I was the spiritual consumer—an observer, not a participant." Do you recognize any of your own attitudes in these admissions? If so, how?

8. Finally, Craig writes: "The church is not here for us. We *are* the church, and we are here *for the world*." How could this attitude change how you feel about other Christ followers and how you interact with your friends who still do not know Christ?

CHAPTER 2
I HAVE TO WORK HARD TO STAY SEXUALLY PURE

Big Idea: Sexual purity is a tough one for Christians—we know we're held to extra-high standards, yet rarely can we talk honestly about our struggles. In our culture, sexual temptations hit us at every turn and compromises are routinely overlooked. What would "not even a hint of sexual immorality" look like in our lives? Craig asks. He advises us to learn to run from temptation, watch what we watch, watch our company, and watch for the moment of decision. We must be willing to confess our sins, and then take "the hard road to purity."

1. Craig writes: "Most people avoid discussing sexual purity, especially around churches. When it *is* discussed, it's generally superficial, out of touch, and watered-down, or it's the other extreme—the heavy-handed, sex-is-bad-and-only-for-procreation-so-whatever-you-do-DON'T-enjoy-it message." Share some of your personal experiences of how sex is (or isn't) dealt with in a church environment.

2. Craig is forthcoming about his sexual past—the wins and the losses. Think back over your own sexual history. (You might consider writing it out—for your use only—to see all in one place any patterns or struggles from your past that might be shaping your beliefs and actions today.) What could your past teach you about how to deal with the challenges you face today?

3. Could you point to a formative experience in your coming-of-age years that still affects your sexuality today? If that experience was positive and healthy, why? If it was negative or hurtful, have you experienced grace and healing, or would you say you're still stuck?

4. If you are already serious about sexual purity in your life, what personal choices or habits have been most helpful to you? What situations or kinds of people put you at greatest risk?

5. Craig quotes 1 Corinthians 10:12: "If you think you are standing firm, be careful that you don't fall!" What guard rails have you put in place in your life to help you stand firm in the area of sexual purity? What ones might need to be added?

6. If you're a parent, what practical, loving steps could you take to protect your children from the pervasive influence of cheap and debasing sex in popular culture?

7. Respond to the following observation by Craig: "One key to sexual purity in my life is consistent, intentional accountability. This isn't a polite, occasional breakfast meeting. Real accountability partners will kick your butt if you go astray. You have to have honest talks on a rigorous schedule."

CHAPTER 3
MOST OF THE TIME I FEEL INCREDIBLY LONELY

Big Idea: In this chapter, Craig addresses the paradox that although God made us to need each other, we can still experience deep loneliness even when we're in genuine relationships. We can experience loneliness—and respond in destructive ways to it—even when we're in a crowd, or in a fulfilling marriage. Loneliness can be intensified because we've put up protective walls between ourselves and others, often because of distrust that originates in past betrayals and hurts. But this kind of disconnected living doesn't work: We become trapped in performing, in distrust, and in thinking no one really cares. God calls us to take risks to let others in.

1. Have you ever found yourself saying something like, "No one knows the real me"? Talk about the circumstances and feelings surrounding that statement.
2. Would you say that loneliness is a significant issue in your life or not? If so, how does it show itself?
3. Do you think people often deal with loneliness in ways that mask its presence—ways like depression, suspicion, bitterness, or busyness? What about you?
4. Craig writes, "Someone said that if you're lonely at the top, it's because you didn't take anyone with you." Do you think certain roles or certain seasons make us especially prone to loneliness? If so, how?
5. Have you had a friend who has helped you relearn trust and openness with others? What was it about their role in your life that was helpful? How could you be that person to someone else?
6. Craig talks about the connection between pride and loneliness—that his pride had been a barrier between him and others. How might pride be blocking you from receiving God's blessings through His people?
7. How could your life change for the better if you invested more intentionally in meaningful friendships?

CHAPTER 4
I HATE PRAYER MEETINGS

Big Idea: Prayer in public feels phony for many and like pure torture for some. Somehow this most intimate spiritual act gets turned into a performance art. And then there's private prayer: If many Christians were honest, they'd have to admit that their personal prayer life is anemic at best. Craig writes about himself and others as people who "genuinely love God but struggle at maintaining a growing and intimate relationship with Him." Craig goes on to share what's been helpful to him in developing his prayer life: get honest with God, take radical risks to trust Him, and learn to live in an attitude of continual prayer.

1. How do you feel about praying in public? What experiences have shaped your attitudes and expectations?

2. Can you identify any dynamics in a typical church prayer meeting that might make authentic prayer harder to come by instead of easier?

3. If you were to take a one-week inventory of your private prayer life, what would the facts reveal? What would you want to change?

4. Honestly, do you think God cares about your concerns? Do you believe He listens and answers your prayers? Talk about how your *actual* beliefs might be influencing how and when you pray.

5. Have you ever gotten rude, angry, or in other ways "unspiritual" toward God in prayer? What happened, and what did you learn from that experience?

6. What creative approaches to praying have been helpful for you?

7. Craig writes: "Any good communication is two-way. Sometimes you need to shut up and listen. God wants to speak to you." How much time do you spend intentionally listening to God? How could you make this a more meaningful part of your relationship with Him?

CHAPTER 5
I WORRY ALMOST ALL THE TIME

Big Idea: "Christians are expected to have great faith in a great God—worrying isn't supposed to be part of our lives, and we feel ashamed when it is," writes Craig. "I know it makes me feel like an absolute spiritual failure. It haunts me and rarely goes away completely. The harsh reality is that even as a Christian, even as a pastor, I worry almost all the time." Progress only comes for chronic worriers, says Craig, when we internalize the truths we say we believe about God's goodness and care, and take practical steps to live in freedom, not fear.

1. How does worrying show itself in your life? For example, at what times of day and in what situations are you most likely to be vulnerable to intense worry?
2. Craig talks about childhood experiences that turned him into a champion worrier. How about you—do any past influences or events come to mind that could be shaping your worry reflex now?

3. Try to list the good things that can come from worrying, then the bad things. On balance, what would you have to gain by learning to worry less and trust more?

4. Craig asks, "Isn't it possible that the very fears the enemy tries to plant in your mind are advertisements for God's good stuff?" What's your response to that intriguing question?

5. What's the connection between our desire to be in control and our impulse to worry? How could a more genuine faith in God change life for "control freaks"?

6. What are the practical steps you could take this week to address two or three worry points that keep surfacing in your life but which you don't usually *do* anything about?

7. "What weight in your life feels like it's 'all you'?" asks Craig. "Take a break. You can rest once you realize that it's all God. Always has been." What would it take to integrate this realization into your daily thinking? If you did, how could your spiritual and emotional life be re-energized?

CHAPTER 6
SOMETIMES I DOUBT GOD

Big Idea: "Is it so unreasonable to expect God to do a few small things to help everyone believe in Him?" asks Craig. Most Christians think that doubts will disappear the minute they're saved, but that's not usually the case. At first we look for God to "magically" make our doubts go away. Then when He doesn't, we feel guilty and disappointed that doubts about Him keep popping up. But the truth is that doubts can become the foundation for a vigorous and authentic faith.

1. Describe your experience of spiritual doubt. In your life has it tended to be an acute reaction to specific events or more of a chronic condition?
2. Craig talks about how he gave God a test to prove His presence and power. Have you had a similar experience? If so, describe it and what you learned.
3. Craig also describes a moment when God's presence became mysteriously, powerfully real. If you have had a similar experience, talk about what it was like and what you learned.
4. "There's a big difference between believing *in* God and *believing* God," Craig writes. Do you agree? If so, what does the distinction mean to you?
5. Would you describe yourself as a *casual* believer, a *convenient* believer, or a *committed* believer? (See the "Breeds of Belief" section, starting on page 126.)
6. What are some of the benefits of acknowledging your doubts and pursuing answers?
7. If you've struggled in the past with whether God is fair, describe your experience, and how your struggle has (or hasn't) been resolved.

CHAPTER 7
I FEEL COMPLETELY INADEQUATE

Big Idea: Despite some public accomplishments, Craig feels that his résumé is one of consistent failure. Feelings of being not smart enough, good enough, or spiritual enough dog him, no matter how hard he tries. But people who feel trapped by their inadequacies forget that "God has enough grace and power to forgive every mistake and correct every flaw," he writes. We need to notice that Jesus picked ordinary men and women to associate with and to follow Him. Craig recommends the advice a friend once gave him: "God doesn't choose the prepared. He prepares the chosen."

1. If you struggle with feelings of inadequacy, describe in which areas those feelings are most likely to strike, and how you tend to respond.

2. Why do you think a good performance seems to bolster our confidence for a shorter period of time than a bad performance or major blunder seems to undermine it?

3. Craig says that prideful people are most often just insecure people wearing a mask of pride. Do you agree? Why or why not?

4. Do you ever find yourself trying to "hide" your inadequacies from God? If so, why? What might be God's actual expectations of you?

5. Craig writes, "God will use you in spite of your insecurities. And He'll often use you where you're *most*

214

insecure." If you have an experience of this in your life, talk about it. What did you learn?

6. Don't believe your fans *or* your critics, suggests Craig. Is this good advice? If so, why, in your opinion?

7. When you have felt your inadequacies and failures most keenly, what truths from God and His Word have been most encouraging?

CHAPTER 8
I STINK AT HANDLING CRITICISM

Big Idea: Craig confesses: "I care too much about what people think. I should be consumed with pleasing God, but I'm often consumed with the impossible—trying to please people." The problem is compounded because most of us are constantly bombarded by negative, critical opinions, he says. How we respond—whether by fight or flight—often doesn't help either. The answer is to come up with practical, doable steps to responding to our critics, and finding our peace in God's steadfast love.

1. Where would you place yourself on the spectrum between "painfully sensitive to criticism" and "blissfully oblivious to criticism"? Are you happy with where you fall on the spectrum? Explain.

2. Identify the person or persons in your life who have tended to be most critical of you, your choices, and your performance. What do you think is driving their

negative opinions? Have you tended to respond to them by *fight* or by *flight?*

3. Craig quotes a verse from Proverbs: "If you listen to constructive criticism, you will be at home among the wise. If you reject criticism, you only harm yourself." Why is it so hard to identify which criticism is constructive? What are some ways to make this judgment call before you hear the criticism itself?

4. If you can recall a time when you answered a criticism and positive results came of it, talk about what happened, and what you could learn?

5. Craig writes, "Hurt people hurt people." Do you agree? How can this observation help us deal with criticism?

6. Have you ever determined to put a stop to all your critical thinking and talking? If so, what has been the result? If not, how do you think that choice could affect your daily experience?

7. "In Christ we are forgiven. In Christ we are secure. In Christ we are free," writes Craig. How can those truths encourage us in the face of unwarranted criticism?

CHAPTER 9
I'M AFRAID OF FAILURE

Big Idea: Craig calls failure his "monster fear." "Whatever our responsibilities are," he writes, "if we take them seriously, we don't want to fail, and if we allow ourselves, we can live daily in fear of our next misstep." That fear can drive us to inaction, to distrusting God, to always playing it safe. Craig describes what he calls "God's Philosophy of Failure": We *will* fail, for example (the challenge is to take good risks). And: Our failures don't define our worth, but they can accomplish good things in our lives. In fact, for the person of faith, playing it safe is not an option. Fortunately, our Father will care for us and empower us as we seek His best.

1. Is fear of failure a "monster" in your life? If so, how does it affect your thoughts, emotions, and decisions?
2. Would you say you're more motivated by the fear of failure or the desire for success? Why?
3. What comes to mind as you read this question from Craig: "What if Jesus took your opportunities…and gave them to someone else?"
4. Craig tells the story of the monkeys in a scientific experiment who learn through second-hand experience not to reach for success (in their case, it was a bunch of bananas). Would you say you grew up in a family or culture that *encouraged* or *discouraged* you to reach for your dreams? Describe your experience and how it affects you today.
5. How could the statement, "Failure is an event, never a person," encourage you and help you take strategic risks?
6. Craig says, "God sometimes accomplishes good results through failure." Have you experienced this in your own life? If so, describe what happened.
7. "You cannot play it safe and please God," writes Craig, citing Hebrews 11:6—"Without faith it is impossible

to please God." How could you apply this huge truth to the fears that threaten you today?

CHAPTER 10
ONE LAST CONFESSION

Big Idea: Craig tells the story of an exotic dancer who decides to reveal her darkest secret to a group of Christ-following friends. "Moments after revealing her most embarrassing secret, Maggie collided head-on with the love of Christ shown through His people." Craig cites that story and his own to encourage the reader to "drop the pose, choose honesty, and get real with God as a way of life."

1. Often it's the experience of someone else's confession—and seeing the loving response that follows—that encourages us to risk getting honest with ourselves and others. Have you had this experience while reading *Dare to Drop the Pose*? Talk about it.

2. What's the worst that could happen to you if you chose to risk honesty, vulnerability, and authenticity…and things went badly? What's the best that could happen? Which decision makes the most sense for your life? Which decision would invite the greatest blessings from God?

3. Craig writes that "getting real isn't just what we *could* do or *should* do—it's what we must do if we're going to

experience the life that Jesus promises." Do you agree with Craig? Why or why not?

4. Visualize how your life could change for the better if you chose to join Craig in his "radical commitment to live the most authentic, transparent, vulnerable life a Christ follower can." Describe what you see? How much do you want it?

5. Are you willing to ask God to help you make your own radical commitment? If not, what do you think might still be holding you back?

6. Craig's closing encouragement is, "Go with the real thing." Take some time to express to God what you want to be real in your life.

7. Write down several practical steps that you feel God is inviting you to take toward honesty and authenticity. Then find a friend with whom you can share your commitments, and who will help you keep them.

Works Cited

1. George Barna. *The Second Coming of the Church*. (Nashville, TN: W Publishing, 2001), p.6.
2. Bella English, "The Secret Life of Boys," *The Boston Globe*, May 12, 2005.
3. Peggy Vaughn. *The Monogamy Myth: A Personal Handbook for Dealing with Affairs, Third Edition*. (New York: Newmarket Press, 2003), p.26.

ACKNOWLEDGMENTS

To everyone who helped with *Dare to Drop the Pose*, thank you for your efforts, expertise, and honesty. You're a great team.

I'm especially grateful for:

Brian Smith—you make my words on paper sound like me, only much better. Thanks for all the hours of hard work. More so, thank you for your growing friendship.

The whole Multnomah crew, including David Kopp, Adrienne Spain, Jason Myhre, Jake Burts, Doug Gabbert, and Kevin Marks, among many others—you're all the "real deal," and it's an honor to partner with you for God's glory.

Brannon, Ali, and Jerry—thanks for reading the manuscript and giving me your candid thoughts. You made the book so much better.

Stretch and Paco Brewsky—you know who you are and how grateful I am for your friendships.

Dad and Mom—thank you for teaching me about unconditional love.

My LifeChurch.tv family—dogs rule and cats drool.

Amy—you'll always be my best friend.

Define Your Vision.
Pursue Your Passion.
Live Your Life on Purpose.

Chazown (pronounced khaw-ZONE) from the Hebrew, meaning a dream, revelation, or vision.

Are you living with purpose and passion? Craig Groeschel invites you on an odyssey to discover and live out your personal Chazown. This one-of-a-kind life planning experience is practical, fresh, and biblically sound, and will transform your relationship with God, your relationships with people, your finances, your health, and your work.

www.chazown.com

Love, sex, and happily ever after?

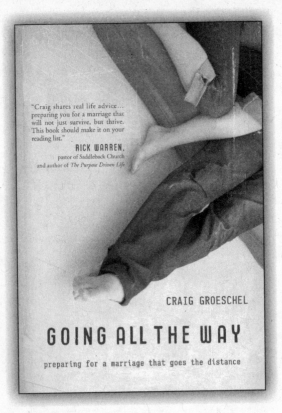

"Craig shares real life advice...
preparing you for a marriage that
will not just survive, but thrive.
This book should make it on your
reading list."

RICK WARREN,
pastor of Saddleback Church
and author of *The Purpose Driven Life*

CRAIG GROESCHEL

GOING ALL THE WAY

preparing for a marriage that goes the distance

"Going all the way" used to mean getting what you want from the opposite sex now...and paying for it later. It's time to redefine.

Whether you're thinking ahead to marriage, are about to be wed, or have been married for a while and want to make changes, Craig Groeschel's *Going All the Way* will guide you through the choices and commitments you need to make now in order to build a strong and vibrant relationship that will go the distance.